GOOD CLEAN

VOLUME 2

FUN

50 MORE NIFTY GAMES
FOR YOUR YOUTH GROUP

TOM FINLEY

Youth Specialties

ZONDERVAN PUBLISHING HOUSE
Grand Rapids, Michigan

GOOD CLEAN FUN Volume 2: More Nifty Games for Your Youth Group

Youth Specialties Books are published by the Zondervan Publishing House, 1415 Lake Drive, S.E., Grand Rapids, Michigan 49506

ISBN 0-310-31651-0

Edited by Dave Lambert

Illustrated by Tom Finley

Printed in the United States of America

89 90 91 92 93 / 10 9 8 7 6 5 4 3 2

Hi! WELCOME TO GOOD CLEAN FUN VOLUME 2

Here are fifty nifty brand-new games wrapped around the word of God. All the games are about Jesus Christ—what He said, what He did and who He is. There's a lot of good game time here, so sharpen up your pencil, crack your knuckles and get ready to enjoy a good clean ton of Good Clean Fun!

Some important notes:

Most of the games require only a pencil, eraser and maybe some scratch paper. Once in awhile you'll need a coin, scissors, paper clip or male elephant . . . no, wait, not the elephant (we just wanted to see if you were paying attention). Anyway, games that require extra items will say so. Each game features all the appropriate Bible verses when possible. But be sure to read along in your own Bible as you play these games.

Need copies for everyone in your group? No problem. Every page is reproducible on any photocopy machine. If you can find a machine that enlarges, you might want to make big copies of some games.

The answers to the more difficult games are found in the "Answer Sheet" section at the back of the book. Now—enjoy learning about Jesus as you have some Good Clean Fun!

TOM FINLEY

Contents

Game #1

In the beginning was the Word, and the Word was with God, and the Word was God. He was with God in the beginning. *(John 1:1,2)*

These verses are talking about Jesus Christ. He is the Word.

The gospel of John was published in the old Greek language of Jesus' day. Our English *word* was, in Greek, *logos*. Perhaps you've heard the term "company logo." We are all familiar with company logos—the famous emblems of fast-food chains, the well-known symbols of cola companies and so forth.

Well, Jesus is God's "company emblem." He represents God here on earth. By being God and by acting like God here on earth, Jesus taught us much of what we know about God the Father.

By playing this simple (but time consuming) game, you can find out how to fill in the blank in this sentence:

Jesus is God's _____ here on earth.

Instructions: The grid you see has hundreds of little boxes formed by the grid lines. If you look closely, you'll notice that most of the boxes have broken walls. Some boxes have one broken wall, some two, three or four. Use your pencil to fill in only the boxes with three broken sides. The filled-in boxes will reveal the solution.

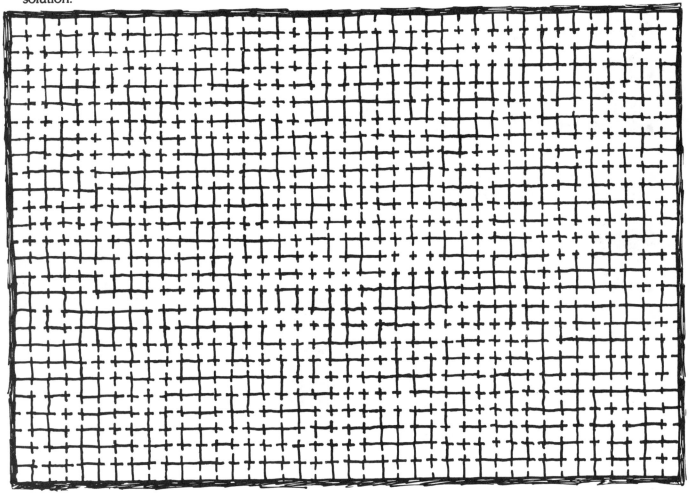

For solution, see page 106.

Game #2 # The Magi Maze!

After Jesus was born in Bethlehem in Judea, during the time of King Herod, Magi from the east came to Jerusalem and asked, "Where is the one who has been born king of the Jews? We saw his star in the east and have come to worship."
(Matthew 2:1,2)

If you correctly work this maze, you can help the Magi (sometimes called the Three Wise Men) find the star they are looking for. There's just one catch: You must decide which star to connect with which Magi! Only the proper ones connect.

The star that lead the Magi to Jesus was a miraculous sign—a sign that Jesus was no ordinary child. As the verses above say, He is a king. Someday He will return to rule.

For solution, see page 106.

The Next-to-Impossible
WORD SEARCH!

Through him all things were made; without him nothing was made that has been made.
(John 1:3)

Jesus made it all! Now, the question is: Can you make it through this game? You see, this is no ordinary word search game. Oh, no. This time, all the words you are looking for in the alphabet square are *scrambled!* The words run only horizontally and vertically. Two have been circled and translated for you as examples. More than one person can play this game by having a race to see who can find the most words in a set time limit.

Search for these things that Jesus made:

EARTH
PEOPLE
CLOUDS
ANIMALS
PLANTS
LIGHT
MOON
STARS
ELECTRICITY
ANGELS
MOUNTAINS
TREES
FISH
ATMOSPHERE
EVERYTHING

```
E E V Y R H T N I G R L J U J K S
R T H X B K F J K L B H F J W D G N
S R H T E A K F J N L E S X T U D F I
O J H G R N K G N R E O G H S E R A
F N A L G S K E E C Y C E O S D S T
S V B H J I P T K I K R E J A Z S V N
E O P E L I R G E F D S N G E S O
W D S W E F R H U O C E F I J I K M
G R T Y W D S U O C L X C H E S D
G T H U K L O P S Q X C H K C F E K I
A Q C L P A T N L I E F S D I I S
D F G T J I K O N A M I A R T L B
E M T S U M O L P E N L F R Y Y H
A O G A T E L R E T A C C I T Y G
R N H T B K F J K L B X F W D G H
S O T S J T A M S O E E R H P F R
O J H R R N K G R E O P H J T R
```

(word-search puzzle grid with the words RHTEA and HFIS circled)

Jesus made all the things you found in the game. If you think it was hard finding them, think how much effort and power it took for Jesus to make them! We have a wonderful Lord!

For solution, see page 106.

11

LIGHT IN DARKNESS!

In him was life, and that life was the light of men. The light shines in the darkness, but the darkness has not understood it. *(John 1:4,5)*

Here's a game of skill that will show you how important it is to live in the light instead of the darkness. Place your pencil point on the cue ball on the billiard table. Close your eyes and try to draw a line that ends on one of the object balls. Open your eyes to see how you did. If you hit the ball, give yourself the number of points shown on the ball. If you missed, subtract 3 points and try again. Do this for all the balls. (To do it right, you should go from ball #1 to ball #15.) If you find this game a bit too easy, draw your lines so they hit the balls and then go into one of the table pockets. That oughta be just about impossible! More than one person can play this game by taking turns.

It would be a lot easier to play this game if you kept your eyes open! In the same way, it's much easier to live a happy, satisfying life if you walk in the light with Jesus Christ. Remember, darkness is the enemy of the one who wants to belong to Jesus Christ. Keep close to Jesus—He will light your path.

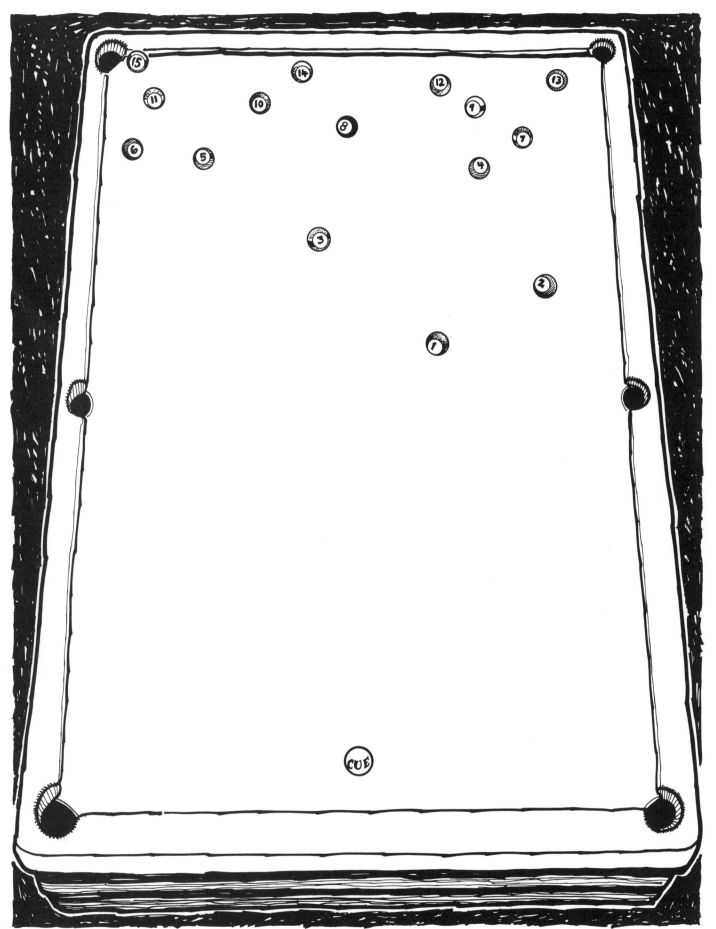

He came to that which was his own, but his own did not receive him. Yet to all who received him, to those who believed in his name, he gave the right to become children of God.

(John 1:11,12)

"Whoever believes in the Son has eternal life, but whoever rejects the Son will not see life, for God's wrath remains on him."

(John 3:36)

These verses make a clear point: To receive eternal life, we must believe in Jesus Christ.

To help yourself remember this important truth, try your hand at this challenger: Your job is to fit all the words

into the grid so that the words properly share letters (like a crossword puzzle). A sample game shows you what we mean.

Words from John 1:11,12; 3:16:

CAME
THAT
WHICH
HIS
BUT
DID
NOT
RECEIVE
YET
ALL
WHO
RECEIVED
HIM
THOSE
BELIEVE
BELIEVED

NAME
GAVE
THE
RIGHT
CHILDREN
GOD
WHOEVER
BELIEVES
HAS
ETERNAL
LIFE
REJECTS
SEE
WRATH
REMAINS

For solution, see page 106.

Sample game:

BOOK
LOOK
LUBE
BAKE

The people came to Moses and said, "We sinned when we spoke against the Lord and against you. Pray that the Lord will take the snakes away from us." So Moses prayed for the people.

The Lord said to Moses, "Make a snake and put it on a pole; anyone who is bitten can look at it and live." So Moses made a bronze snake and put it up on a pole. Then when anyone was bitten by a snake and looked at the bronze snake, he lived.

(Numbers 21:7-9)

"Just as Moses lifted up the snake in the desert, so the Son of Man must be lifted up, that everyone who believes in him may have eternal life."

(John 3:14,15)

A couple of strange Bible passages, right? People are dying from poison snakebites, so God tells Moses to hang a bronze snake on a pole so whoever sees it will be cured. Then Jesus says that He will also be lifted up like the bronze snake so people can have eternal life.

Jesus was talking about His crucifixion. You see, Jesus died so that we may live. He paid the penalty for our sins. As Jesus said, everyone who believes in Him is saved.

To help you remember the story of the snakes and the importance of Christ's death on the cross, try this unique maze. You must draw a line from **START** to **ETERNAL LIFE IN CHRIST.** But it's not easy to do—your line must always travel from the tail of a snake to the head (think of the snake as an arrow pointing the direction). Also, your line must always follow the snakes in numerical order: 1,2,3,1,2,3,1,2,3 and so on. The snakes cross over and under each other. Good luck and fangs a lot.

Snake bit? The solution is on page 106.

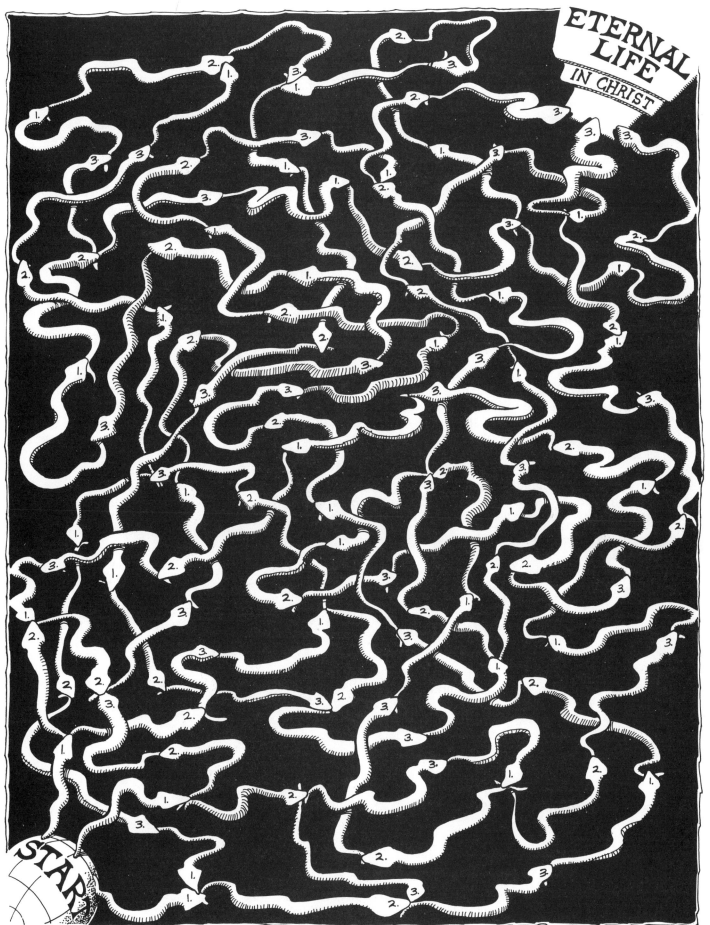

ETERNAL
LIFE
IN CHRIST

START

17

As Jesus was walking beside the Sea of Galilee, he saw two brothers, Simon called Peter and his brother Andrew. They were casting a net into the lake, for they were fishermen. "Come, follow me," Jesus said, "and I will make you fishers of men." At once they left their nets and followed him. *(Matthew 4:18-20)*

They started out catching fish, but they ended up catching people with the good news of Jesus Christ. You can catch fish and people by playing this tough little game. Draw a pencil line from the fishing pole to the bait bucket—your pencil line must follow the fishing line. Along the way, catch as many fish and people as you can. Two important rules: Your pencil line can never cross itself and you cannot use the same segment of fishing line more than once. The sample game gives you an idea how this works.

When you've got as many fish and people as you can catch, add up your score. People count as two points, fish are only one. Compare your score to the **SCORE CARD** at the bottom of the game. Or two people can play by playing two games and comparing scores.

Sample game:

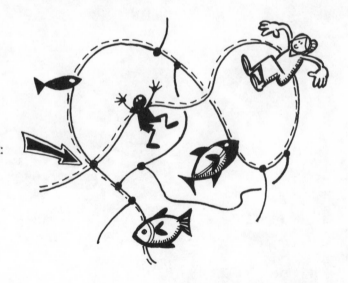

This is against the rules—the lines cannot connect:

A solution is shown on page 106.

If you have been worrying about fishing for people—telling them about Jesus, that is—remember one simple rule: Just tell your friends what you know. If all you know is that Jesus is your Savior, then tell them about that. God will honor your efforts and good things will happen! Give it a try.

CROWDS AND KINDS!

News about him spread all over Syria, and people brought to him all who were ill with various diseases, those suffering severe pain, the demon-possessed, those having seizures, and the paralyzed, and he healed them.

(Matthew 4:24)

At this time in Jesus' public life, huge crowds followed Him almost everywhere He went. These multitudes contained every kind of person imaginable, from sick beggars to stuffy religious leaders.

Today, all people are still welcome to follow Christ. This word search game contains 2 words describing the sort of people who can come to the Lord today. We won't tell you what words to look for—it's up to you to figure them out. The words run vertically, horizontally, diagonally—and they sometimes twist and turn! As you work, see if you can find one or more words that describe *you*.

HI MOM!

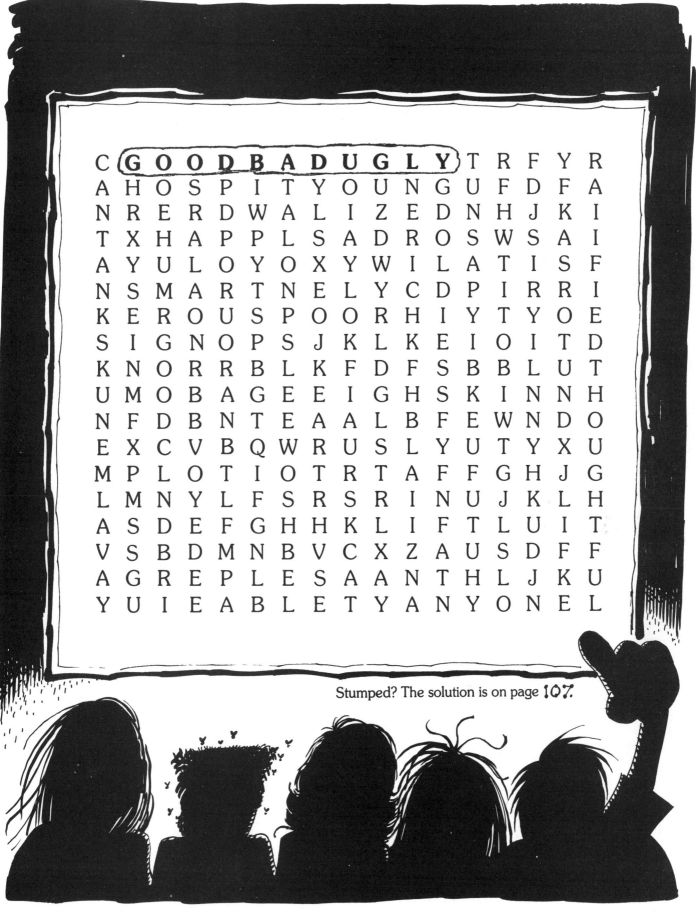

C (**G O O D B A D U G L Y**) T R F Y R
A H O S P I T Y O U N G U F D F A
N R E R D W A L I Z E D N H J K I
T X H A P P L S A D R O S W S A I
A Y U L O Y O X Y W I L A T I S F
N S M A R T N E L Y C D P I R R I
K E R O U S P O O R H I Y T Y O E
S I G N O P S J K L K E I O I T D
K N O R R B L K F D F S B B L U T
U M O B A G E E I G H S K I N D H
N F D B N T E A A L B F E W N D O
E X C V B Q W R U S L Y U T Y X U
M P L O T I O T R T A F F G H J G
L M N Y L F S R S R I N U J K L H
A S D E F G H H K L I F T L U I T
V S B D M N B V C X Z A U S D F F
A G R E P L E S A A N T H L J K U
Y U I E A B L E T Y A N Y O N E L

Stumped? The solution is on page 107.

21

Now when he saw the crowds, he went up on a mountainside and sat down. His disciples came to him, and he began to teach them.

(Matthew 5:1,2)

Ready for a real challenge? Play this game based on what Jesus taught in Matthew 1:3-11. Jesus was comforting His listeners by explaining to them that God will bless them in troubled times as well as in good times. The first part of each blessing is on the left side of the maze and the second part of each is on the right side. You are to connect the correct parts by drawing lines along the maze paths. The parts are listed in proper order—connect 1 with 1, 2 with 2, and so on. (We've paired the blessings to keep the game from being too hard.)

Important: The lines you draw must never touch or cross (except on paths that obviously cross over or under each other). You cannot use the same segment of path twice. Some people find this kind of game relatively easy—but most don't!

In what ways has God blessed you lately? Take a moment to think about it. Then say a little prayer of thanks to Him.

Can't believe this maze can be solved? It can—see the solution on page **107**

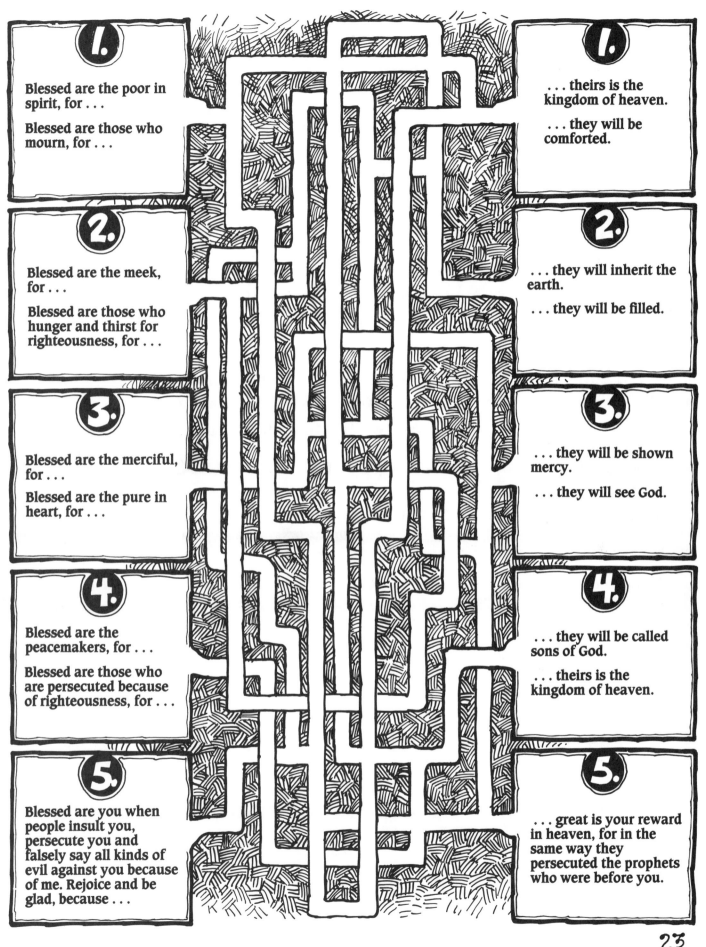

1. Blessed are the poor in spirit, for . . .

Blessed are those who mourn, for . . .

2. Blessed are the meek, for . . .

Blessed are those who hunger and thirst for righteousness, for . . .

3. Blessed are the merciful, for . . .

Blessed are the pure in heart, for . . .

4. Blessed are the peacemakers, for . . .

Blessed are those who are persecuted because of righteousness, for . . .

5. Blessed are you when people insult you, persecute you and falsely say all kinds of evil against you because of me. Rejoice and be glad, because . . .

1. . . . theirs is the kingdom of heaven.

. . . they will be comforted.

2. . . . they will inherit the earth.

. . . they will be filled.

3. . . . they will be shown mercy.

. . . they will see God.

4. . . . they will be called sons of God.

. . . theirs is the kingdom of heaven.

5. . . . great is your reward in heaven, for in the same way they persecuted the prophets who were before you.

23

Salt and Light Rate-O-Meter!

"**You are the salt of the earth. But if the salt loses its saltiness, how can it be made salty again? It is no longer good for anything, except to be thrown out and trampled by men.**

"**You are the light of the world. A city on a hill cannot be hidden. Neither do people light a lamp and put it under a bowl. Instead they put it on its stand, and it gives light to everyone in the house. In the same way, let your light shine before men, that they may see your good deeds and praise your Father in heaven.**" *(Matthew 5:13-16)*

Jesus wants us to have a positive effect on this world. As He put it, we are to be salty and bright as lights.

So how are you doing? Are you living up to Christ's desires? Let's find out. Starting at the bottom of the Rate-O-Meter with question #1, answer each question yes or no. Use your pencil to follow the path your answers lead you on. (The sample game shows you what we mean.) The path will lead you higher and higher until you reach the top level. There you will find your **SALT AND LIGHT RATING.** If more than one person plays, you can compare your ratings. But honesty is a must!

8 If a non-Christian saw your Bible, would you feel no embarrassment?

7 Have you ever played a favorite Christian album loud enough for non-Christians to hear?

6 Do you invite friends to youth group events?

5 Would you welcome a chance to go on a summer missionary trip?

4 Do you pray for your friends?

3 Does God know you're a Christian?

2 Does your family know you're a Christian?

1 Do your school pals know you're a Christian?

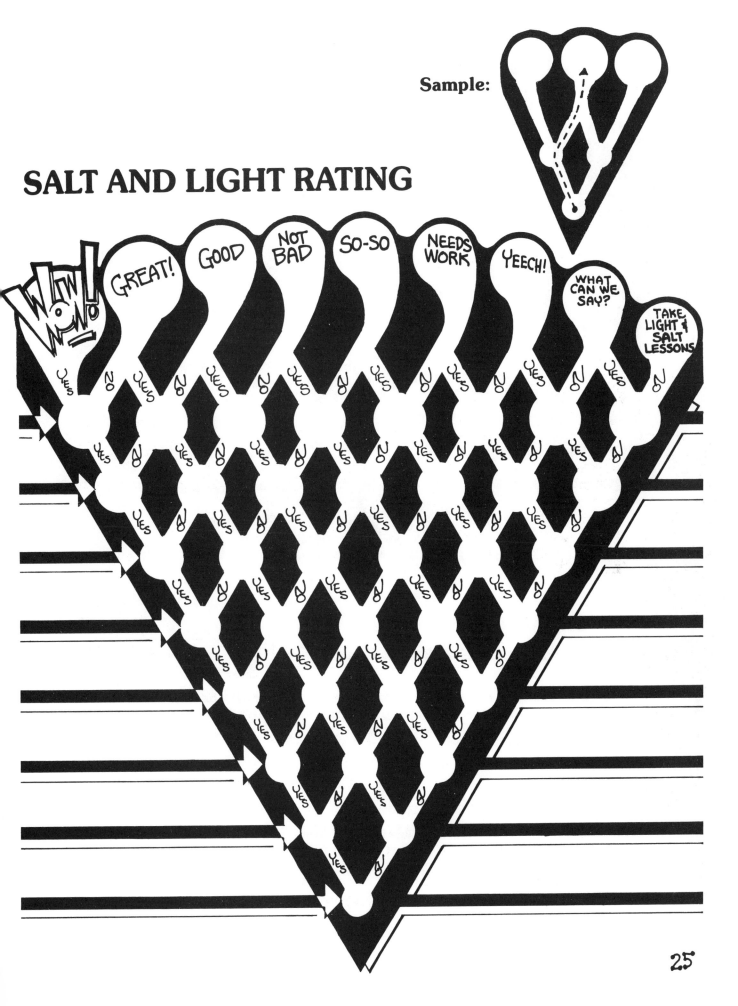

HOW'S THAT GO AGAIN?

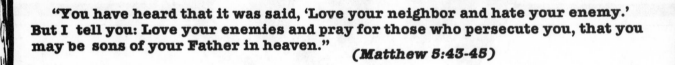

"You have heard that it was said, 'Love your neighbor and hate your enemy.' But I tell you: Love your enemies and pray for those who persecute you, that you may be sons of your Father in heaven." *(Matthew 5:43-45)*

One of the things that set Jesus apart from the other teachers of His day was His radical stance on love. He taught that we are to love even our enemies.

Perhaps the most famous passage in all the Bible is 1 Corinthians 13. It's all about love and is sometimes known as the Love Chapter. We have printed part of 1 Corinthians 13 for you—er, but there's just one problem. Somebody messed it up. Some of the important words have been changed. Your mission is to figure out what words were changed and to put the chapter right again. And if we find out who did this awful deed, we'll squash the little cree—oops! Looks like we need to remember the words of our Lord!

1 Corinthians 13:4-8
(Messed Up Version):

Love is usually patient. Love is kind of nice. It does not envy, except when somebody comes along with a better tan. It does not boast much, but it is proud. It is not rude (table manners don't count), it is not self-seeking, it is not easily angered, though it does keep records of wrongs. Love does not delight in evil but rejoices with the angels. It always protects, always trusts, always hopes, almost always perseveres. Love rarely fails.

The Messed Up Version is pathetic—but so is the tiny amount of love we Christians sometime seem to have in our hearts. This world needs to see much more of the kind of love Jesus commanded us to have. Read the real 1 Corinthians 13. You'll find the correct version of verses 4-8 on the Answer Sheet, page 107. Or read it in your own Bible.

The ACME Auto-Pray!

"And when you pray, do not keep on babbling like pagans, for they think they will be heard because of their many words. Do not be like them, for your Father knows what you need before you ask him." *(Matthew 6:7,8)*

Jesus prayed. The Bible records many times when He got away by Himself on a lonely hillside to pray, stayed up all night in prayer, prayed aloud for the disciples' benefit and so on. He talked to God the Father and so should we. If you haven't yet developed the habit of talking to God a set amount of time each day, your spiritual life is suffering. Prayer is power.

What? You say you haven't got a good habit of daily prayer? We are shocked! But never fear—the **ACME Auto-Pray** is here! Here's how it works: The cards you see list ten things that someone might pray for another person. Cut the cards out. Shuffle all the #1 cards and place them face down in a pile. Do the same for the #2 and #3 cards, so that you have three separate stacks. Now draw one card from each stack and place them in numerical order: #1, #2, #3. The cards will form a prayer—one that you might like to pray today. Actually, you probably won't want to: there are exactly 1000 possible prayer combinations, and about 999 of them are dumb. Frankly, we think you'll find the **ACME Auto-Pray** is a waste of time. It's much wiser to just talk to God the way you want to. Make a habit of it everyday.

Cut out these cards:

I pray that no one will break into your	house	while you are gone.	I pray that you can find some bucks in your	drawer	so we can hit the movies.
I pray that your mom won't hit you with a	frying pan	on your head.	I pray that you can get rid of that huge	zit	before the prom.
I pray that the doctors find a	pill	to cure your warts.	I pray that you don't bite off your	little brother's head	despite what your brother did to your clothes.
I pray that they won't tow away your	car	even though it's broken down in my driveway.	I pray that you can shove your	front tooth	back in your mouth.
I pray that you can catch the	long bomb	and win the big game.	I pray that you won't find a worm in your	salad	and throw up.

The Slow Puzzler!

"But when you _____, put oil on your head and wash your face, so that it will not be obvious to men that you are _____, but only to your Father, who is unseen; and your Father, who sees what is done in secret, will reward you."
(Matthew 6:17,18)

Anybody who has been a Christian for even a short time is aware that there are certain things we must do to grow spiritually mature—things like prayer, checkin' out what the Bible says, hanging around with other Christians and so on. But in the passage above, Jesus mentions a thing that many Christians don't do. If you know your Bible pretty well, you know how to fill in the blanks. But if you don't, solve the mystery by playing our little word game. You'll find a good thing to do when you want to get serious with the Lord. (The second blank in the verse above is another form of the answer in the puzzle.) For more information on the subject, ask your youth pastor or other respected Christian.

To make this game a bit tougher, we've done two things. First, we made some of the picture clues a mite difficult to guess. Second, the answer comes out scrambled—you'll have to unscramble the letters to find the word.

The solution is on page 107.

"Do not store up for yourselves treasures on earth, where moth and rust destroy, and where thieves break in and steal. But store up for yourselves treasures in heaven, where moth and rust do not destroy, and where thieves do not break in and steal. For where your treasure is, there your heart will be also."

(Matthew 6:19-21)

Jesus is talking about materialism. Don't get caught in the quicksand of possessions, He says. Instead, earn rewards in heaven by living the way He wants us to here on earth. Some things He wants us to do are listed on the treasure chests you see on the game board.

To help you remember to keep your heart on the things of heaven rather than the things of earth, we present this little test of skill. Here's what you do: Place two pennies on the bowling alley as shown. By hitting one penny with the other (see illustration), you are to "bowl" for the treasure chests. When your penny lands on a chest, you win points. Give yourself 10 points for a hit. Subtract 3 points for a miss, 5 points for a gutter ball. Two or more can also play this game. Play until all treasures have been won.

Hit penny like this:

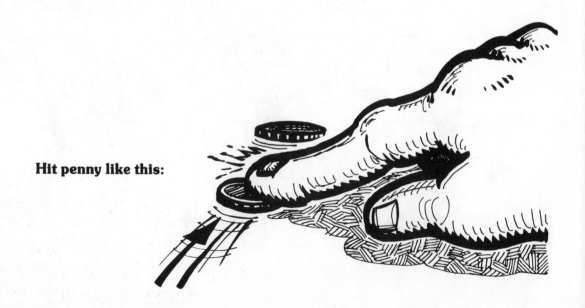

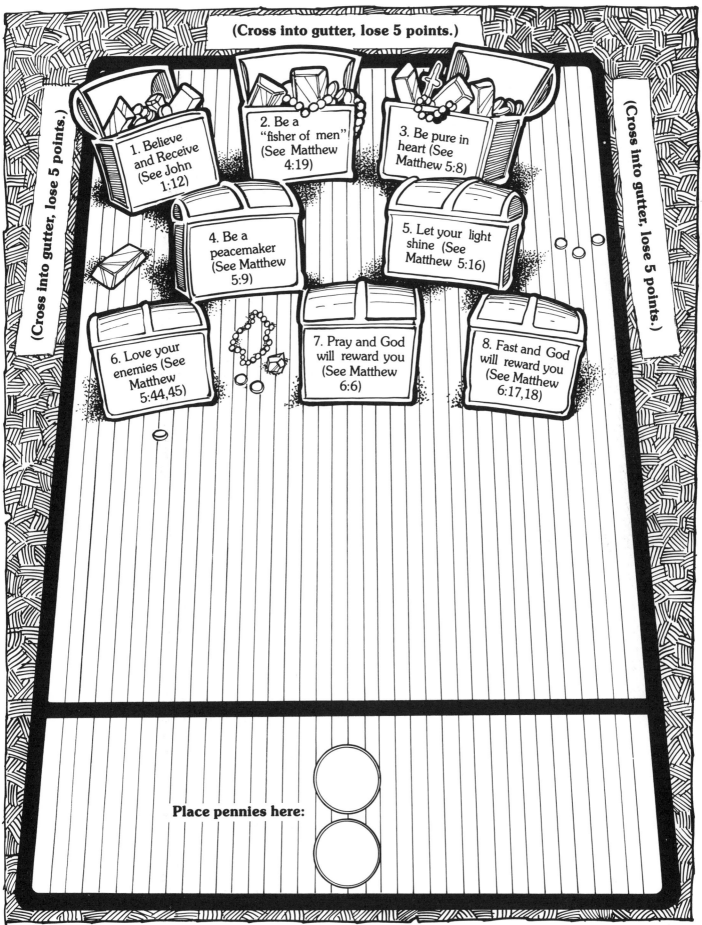

GOING DOTTY!

"No one can serve two masters. Either he will hate the one and love the other, or he will be devoted to one and despise the other. You cannot serve both God and Money."

(Matthew 6:24)

That's clear enough, isn't it? You can either live for Jesus or you can live for the world—but you can't do both. Or maybe you can, if you can do what the solution to this fold-in tells you to do.

Fold along dotted lines until the arrows meet.

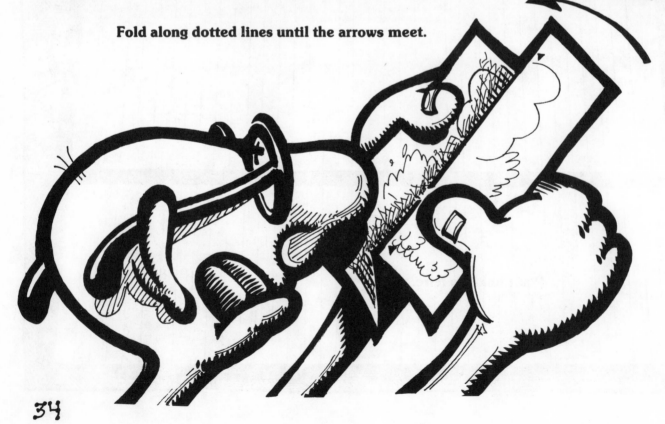

LUCKY DUCK!

"Look at the birds of the air; they do not sow or reap or store in barns, and yet your heavenly Father feeds them. Are you not much more valuable than they?"

(Matthew 6:26)

There's a secret message in this game. It's pretty easy to find—if you don't mind going blind doing it. Simply follow the strings from the birds to the nests. Take the first letter of each bird's name and write it in the attached nest. When you are done, the nests will spell out an important thought based on Matthew 6:26. Keep the thought in mind next time you don't feel so hot.

LOON

TOUCAN

OLD CHICKEN

ALBATROSS

DOVE

BLUE-FOOTED BOOBY

BLUE PAINT

AMERICAN COOT

UGLY DUCKLING

LARRY

ATLANTIC MURRE

EGRET

VELVET SCOTER

GULL

UNCLE DONALD

YELLOW-NAPED AMAZON

EMPEROR PENGUIN

OSTRICH

OWL

RHEA

DOT THE EYES!

"Do not judge, or you too will be judged. For in the same way you judge others, you will be judged, and with the measure you use, it will be measured to you.

"Why do you look at the speck of sawdust in your brother's eye and pay no attention to the plank in your own eye? How can you say to your brother, 'Let me take the speck out of your eye,' when all the time there is a plank in your own eye? You hypocrite, first take the plank out of your own eye, and then you will see clearly to remove the speck from your brother's eye."

(Matthew 7:15)

When we judge others (by thinking we are better than they), it's like trying to get a piece of sawdust out of someone's eye while we have a couple of logs blocking our own vision. If you'll work this dot-to-dot game, you'll see what can happen when you try to cut through another person's little problem when you haven't handled your own. Yeah, we know dot-to-dots are for kids, but we think you'll find the effort worth it.

IT'S A Gift!

"Ask and it will be given to you; seek and you will find; knock and the door will be opened to you. For everyone who asks receives; he who seeks finds; and to him who knocks, the door will be opened."

(Matthew 7:7,8)

There are two ways you can receive good gifts, find what you're looking for and get the door open to a good life. The best way is to ask, seek and knock by trusting God in habitual prayer. The other way is to work this puzzling maze. On second thought, the game won't help. Just take your requests to God. He comes through every time.

Instructions: Your job is to connect the people who are asking, seeking and knocking on the left side of the maze with the things they are looking for on the right side. Be sure to match the proper people to the correct things. The lines you draw cannot touch or cross (except on paths that obviously cross over and under each other). Also, you cannot use the same segment of path more than once. If you chump out, the answer is on page 107.

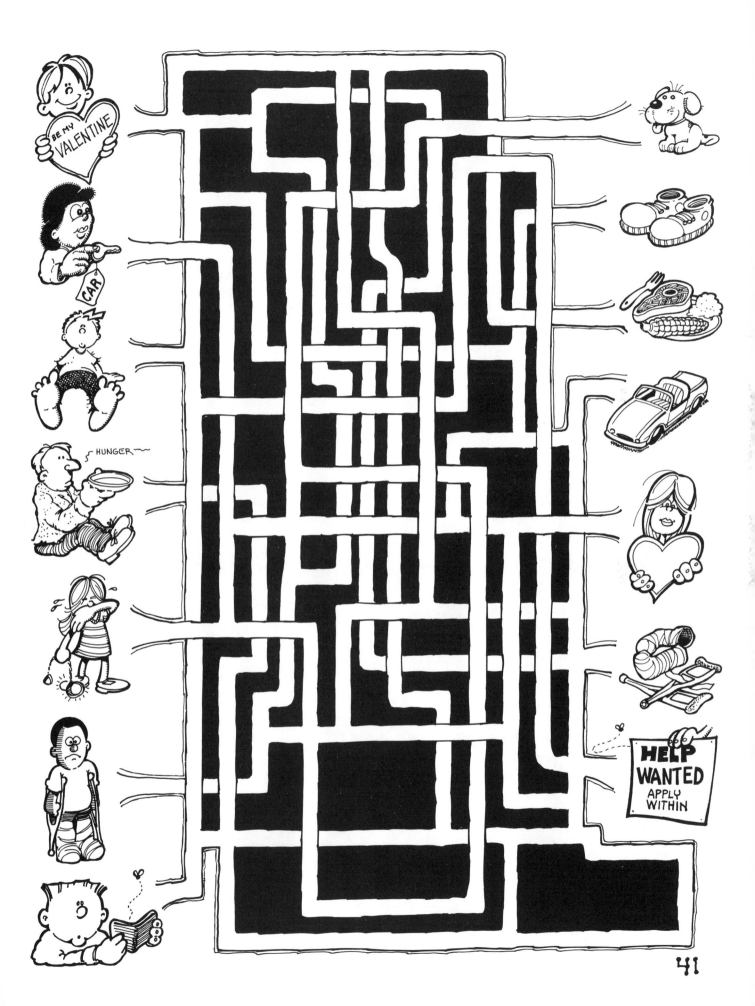

PIG OUT!

When he arrived at the other side in the region of the Gadarenes, two demon-possessed men coming from the tombs met him. They were so violent that no one could pass that way. "What do you want from us, Son of God?" they shouted. "Have you come here to torture us before the appointed time?"

Some distance from them a large herd of pigs was feeding. The demons begged Jesus, "If you drive us out, send us into the herd of pigs."

He said to them, "Go!" So they came out and went into the pigs, and the whole herd rushed down the steep bank into the lake and died in the water. Those tending the pigs ran off, went into the town and reported all this, including what had happened to the demon-possessed men. Then the whole town went out to meet Jesus. And when they saw him, they pleaded with him to leave their region. *(Matthew 8:28-34)*

Jesus was and is a powerful figure. Imagine the astonishment that people felt when they saw Him deal with these poor demon-possessed men. It must have been a truly amazing experience to see Jesus clashing with the armies of Satan right there in the sleepy countryside.

We still need that kind of power today. Satan is real and dangerous. But we don't have to worry, for Jesus is our protector.

But we do have one question: If the demons went into the pigs, and the pigs drowned in the lake, where did all those demons end up? You can find a tongue-in-cheek answer by using your pencil to shade in all the pigs that have frowns on their faces.

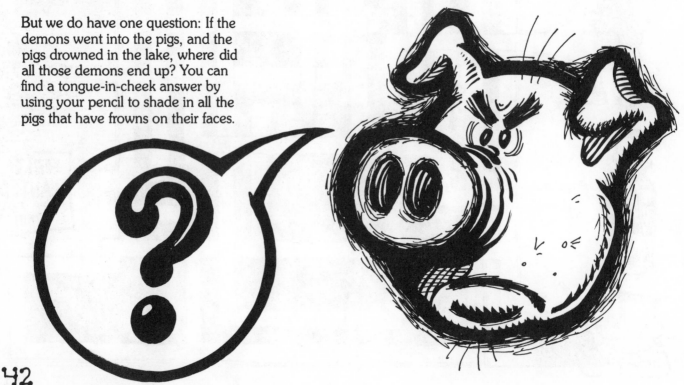

43

BLANK VERSE!

Jesus went through all the towns and villages, teaching in their synagogues, preaching the good news of the kingdom and healing every disease and sickness. When he saw the crowds, he had compassion on them, because they were harassed and helpless, like sheep without a shepherd. Then he said to his disciples, "The harvest is plentiful but the workers are few. Ask the Lord of the harvest, therefore, to send workers into his harvest field." *(Matthew 9:35-38)*

"Do you not say, 'Four months and then the harvest'? I tell you, open your eyes and look at the fields! They are ripe for harvest. Even now the reaper draws his wages, even now he harvests the crop for eternal life, so that the sower and the reaper may be glad together." *(John 4:35,36)*

The field is the world, the workers are the servants of God and the harvest is people who gain eternal life because they come to Jesus in faith.

Here's a chance to check your poetic talent. Got any? Let's find out. Our poem is based on the verses above. We left some of the key words out of the stanzas—you figure out what you think they should be. Our version is found on page 108.

"Send me some workers,"
Said the man into the phone;
"It's time to reap the harvest,
And I'm here all _____."

"Send me Larry, Moe or Curly Joe,
Or anyone you can find;
"I must reap the harvest;
I'm really in a _____."

"Well now," came the slow reply,
"Let's see what I can _____;
"I'll contact some good workers,
And send you out a _____."

So he got hold of some old guy,
A friend that he once _____;
But the guy said, "I can't come to work,
'Cause I'm down with the _____."

He tried again and got in touch,
With a girl out by the _____;
She would have helped out if she could,
But she was on her coffee _____.

"This is stupid," growled the dude,
Who decided to be wiser;
But the next clod said, "No, I won't work—
But I'll be _____."

In an angry rage then, this man called
Everyone around the _____;
But nobody answered when he called.
(They were all on a _____.)

"You must send me someone super quick,"
said the man out in his _____;
"If you don't find me someone now,
I'll see that you are _____."

So humbly the man bowed and prayed,
That God would send just any _____;
You can guess what happened next, can't you?
Just like that He _____.

So a little boy arrived for work,
All happiness and _____;
Until he took a good look at
The field, which stretched for _____.

He picked and picked and picked and picked,
Until the sun turned _____;
He piled up the harvest tall,
Then this is what he _____:

"There's way too much to do here,
More than I can on my _____;
"So send me out some workers,
For I'm here all _____."

You may not think that you could offer much to the Lord as a worker or servant. But you can. He has a place for everyone, and if you want to be used for a good purpose by Him, He'll be glad to set you up in business. Ask your youth pastor if there is anything you can do around church. You'll probably get more than you can handle!

HOLY HANDLES!

He called his twelve disciples to him and gave them authority to drive out evil spirits and to heal every disease and sickness.

(Matthew 10:1)

Just for fun, we've thrown in a pop quiz—a test of your Bible knowledge and memory. Here's the question: What are the names of the 12 disciples mentioned in the verse above?

If you don't know—and we don't expect you to—you can find out by solving this tough little teaser. Here's the deal: We have taken each name and split it into two parts. Then we took the parts and shuffled 'em up and stuck 'em back together in the wrong order. In other words, the first part of one guy's name is attached to the last part of another guy's name. You have to decide where to split the messed up names and get them back in the right order. Think you can handle that? If you can't handle those disciples' handles, the real handles are on page **108**—or just check out Matthew 10:2-4 .

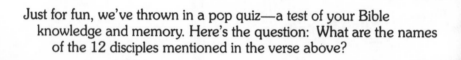

SIDAEUS
JATHEW
JOTER
THADMON
PHIHN
JUREW
PEOMAS
BARTDAS
MATHOLOMEW
ANDMES
THES
JAMLIP

Water Lot of Fun!

Now there is in Jerusalem near the Sheep Gate a pool, which in Aramaic is called Bethesda and which is surrounded by five covered colonnades. Here a great number of disabled people used to lie—the blind, the lame, the paralyzed—and they waited for the moving of the waters. From time to time an angel of the Lord would come down and stir up the waters. The first one into the pool after each such disturbance would be cured of whatever disease he had. One who was there had been an invalid for thirty-eight years. When Jesus saw him lying there and learned that he had been in this condition for a long time, he asked him, "Do you want to get well?"

"Sir," the invalid replied, "I have no one to help me into the pool when the water is stirred. While I am trying to get in, someone else goes down ahead of me."

Then Jesus said to him, "Get up! Pick up your mat and walk." At once the man was cured; he picked up his mat and walked. *(John 5:2-9)*

This is a strange story. It's strange because we don't often hear of angels making bubbles in water so that sick people can be healed. However, Jesus did what He always does: He met someone in need and took care of his troubles. The sick man had been waiting a lot of years; Jesus came along and cured him.

Things looked very bleak for that poor man. But Jesus changed his life. This game may help you remember that when things look bleak, Jesus can make everything right for you.

Instructions: Notice the sick man in the middle of the game board (he's the one wearing the snorkel). Your mission is to help him get to the water so he can be healed. You lead him to the water by drawing a line from him to the pool. As you spin the paper clip spinner (see the drawing), it will tell you how to draw your line. For example, if it says "2 North," you extend your line two spaces up. By using the spinner, your line will wander around the game board.

As your line wanders, it will probably hit some obstacles. Each time your line runs into or over an obstacle, the sick man gets weaker. If you hit three obstacles, you must start over with a new line. The obstacles are the other people, the walls, buildings and so forth. If you run off the game board, move your line two spaces inward and try again.

You can play this game alone or with a friend.
(Two players draw two separate lines.)

You'll need a pencil and paper clip to play this game. Use the pencil and paper clip as shown in the drawing to form a spinner.

Place pencil and paper clip as shown. Flick paper clip with finger. Whichever space is mostly covered by the clip is the course to follow.

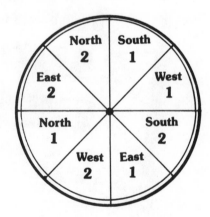

Now that you've tried the game: As you can see, it takes a bit of luck to win this one. The sick man (the real one) was probably hoping some good luck would come his way so that he could become well. But luck isn't the answer. Jesus is the answer. If you are facing problems that seem nearly impossible to solve, turn to the Lord. He's in the solving business.

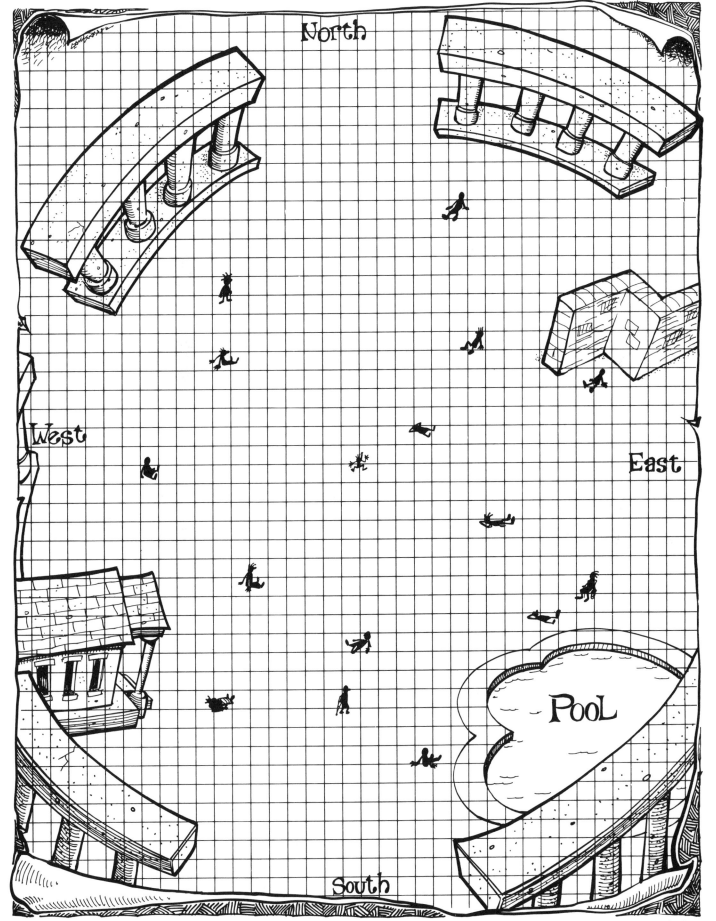

North

West

East

Pool

South

49

Scriptures!

"You diligently study the Scriptures because you think that by them you possess eternal life. These are the Scriptures that testify about me, yet you refuse to come to me to have life." (John 5:39,40)

When He spoke these words, Jesus was talking to a bunch of guys who prided themselves on their knowledge of the Old Testament Scriptures. But just like many people today, they read but they did not follow.

You see, it's possible to read the Bible and still not understand it. Just for fun, here are some important truths from the Bible. They've been scrambled to make them difficult to understand. But if you decipher them, they'll reveal essential truths that—if believed and followed—can change the world.

These two verses have had each word scrambled:

"I LETL UOY HTE RUHTT, EEVHWRO AEHSR YM RDOW NDA SEEEILVB MHI HWO ENST EM SAH TEENRLA FLIE NDA LIWL TON EB NNCMDEODE; EH SHA SCOSRDE VREO MFOR ETADH OT FIEL." John 5:24

"I LTEL OYU HET RTHTU, A MIET SI NGMICO NDA SAH WON MEOC NHEW HET ADED WLIL EARH HET IVOEC FO TEH OSN FO DOG NDA STOEH HOW REAH LLWI VIEL." John 5:25

Too easy? OK, try these on for size. These verses have each had the order of their words rearranged:

BE SALVATION ELSE, IS NAME HEAVEN MEN TO FOUND ONE IN NO THERE FOR WE NO IS UNDER GIVEN WHICH MUST OTHER BY SAVED. Acts 4:12

IF DO HIS HEAR HARDEN YOU YOUR VOICE, TODAY, NOT HEARTS. Hebrews 4:7

NO NOW THOSE FOR WHO CHRIST THEREFORE, CONDEMNATION ARE IS IN THERE JESUS.
Romans 8:1

OK, let's try one more test. If you can get these, consider yourself a genius. These verses have had all the vowels (A, E, I, O, U, Y) replaced by other letters. Each vowel is replaced by two consonants. Good luck!

THLL SCRPRPTLMRSH PRS GSSD-BRSHTHTHSHD THND PRS LMSSHFLML FSSR TSHTHCHPRNG, RSHBLMKPRNG, CSSRRSHCTPRNG THND TRTHPRNPRNG PRN RPRGHTSHSSLMSNSHSS, SSS THTHT THSH MTHN SSF GSSD MTHGH BSH THSSRSSLMGHLGH SHQLMPRPPSHD FSSR SHVSHRGH GSSSSD WSSRK. 2 Timothy 3:16,17

FBBR THRT WBBRD BBF GBBD HSS LHSVHSNG TTND TTCTHSVRT. SHTTRPRTR THTTN TTNRB DBBBRBLRT-TBDGTBD SWHVRD, PLT PTBNTBTRRSTTBS TBVTBN THV DPLVPLDPLNG SHVGQL RSND SPPLRPLT, JHVPLNTS STND MCHRRCHW; CKT JRRDGLSS THLS THCHRRGHTS STND STTTCKTRRDLSS CHF THLS HLSSTRT. Hebrews 4:12

The Bible is not an easy book to understand. If you tend to avoid reading your own Bible because you find it confusing, we recommend that you try a couple of things. Get involved with your youth group's Bible studies—you can ask questions and learn great stuff. Also, get an easy-to-read Bible. Some Bibles are much easier to understand than others, so you can probably find one that will suit your needs.

You've undoubtedly been told that Bible reading is necessary to Christian growth and maturity. You'll see how true that is when you start to make exciting discoveries about God as you stick your nose in His book.

The solutions are on page 108. Or look up the verses in your Bible.

The  of Discipleship!

As they were walking along the road, a man said to him, "I will follow you wherever you go."

Jesus replied, "Foxes have holes and birds of the air have nests, but the Son of Man has no place to lay his head." **(Luke 9:57,58)**

Large crowds were traveling with Jesus, and turning to them he said: "If anyone comes to me and does not hate his father and mother, his wife and children, his brothers and sisters—yes, even his own life—he cannot be my disciple. And anyone who does not carry his cross and follow me cannot be my disciple." **(Luke 14:25-27)**

"Anyone who loves his father or mother more than me is not worthy of me; anyone who loves his son or daughter more than me is not worthy of me; and anyone who does not take up his cross and follow me is not worthy of me. Whoever finds his life will lose it, and whoever loses his life for my sake will find it."

(Matthew 10:37-39)

What is discipleship? In the Christian's case, it's a solid commitment to follow and be with the Lord. But it costs. In Luke 9:57,58 above, Jesus tells a guy that He doesn't stay in the finest hotels; if the man wants to follow Him he better plan on some rough times. In the other two passages, Jesus claims that our love for Him must far exceed our love for our families or even for ourselves. He also says that we better be prepared to use that cross.

This crossword puzzle features many of the words from these things that Jesus said (quoted above). As you work the puzzle, take the time to think about the meaning of the words and the cost of your decision to belong to Jesus. It takes a strong commitment—but you can do it, because God is on your side! If you can't do the game, the solution is on page 109.

ACROSS

2. Transport
4. Fowls
5. Married woman
7. Throngs
9. Misplace
10. Not able
13. Whichever place
14. Bird abodes
18. En route
19. On top of the shoulders
21. Female siblings
23. Put
26. Accompanying
27. Cares for
28. Negatory
29. I
30. Male siblings
32. Not odd
33. Carries out

DOWN

1. Cruciform
2. Youngsters
3. Mine
6. Dog-like animal
8. Person which
9. Exists
11. Atmosphere
12. Whirling
13. Deserving
15. Acquire
16. Strolling
17. Position
19. Cavities
20. Anybody
22. Rescues (A word used in other versions of the Bible for "finds")
24. Patriarch
25. Arrives
27. Big
28. Same as 28 ACROSS
29. Matriarch
31. Also

IT WAS A DARK AND STORMY NIGHT!

After this the Lord appointed seventy-two others and sent them two by two ahead of him to every town and place he was about to go.

The seventy-two returned with joy and said, "Lord, even the demons submit to us in your name."

He replied, "I saw Satan fall like lightning from heaven."

(Luke 10:1,17,18)

The disciples of Christ were stoked because even the evil spirits had to back off in Christ's name. Jesus told His followers that He had been watching Satan fall like lightning striking the ground—a figurative way of saying Satan was being defeated.

What does Satan say when someone like you gets together with Jesus to fight him? Work this maze to find the answer. The correct path from the start to finish will contain a few letters. The letters spell the answer to our question.

The solution to the maze is on page 109.

55

THE NAME GAME!

"I have given you authority to trample on snakes and scorpions and to overcome all the power of the enemy; nothing can harm you. However, do not rejoice that the spirits submit to you, but rejoice that your names are written in heaven."

(Luke 10:19,20)

If God has written your name down on the roll of heaven's citizens, you've got it made! But what happens if your name isn't written down in heaven? You can learn that answer by working our little word/picture game shown on the computer screen.

The solution is on page 109.

Martha, Martha, Quite Contrary!

As Jesus and his disciples were on their way, he came to a village where a woman named Martha opened her home to him. She had a sister called Mary, who sat at the Lord's feet listening to what he said. But Martha was distracted by all the preparations that had to be made. She came to him and asked, "Lord, don't you care that my sister has left me to do the work by myself? Tell her to help me!"

"Martha, Martha," the Lord answered, "You are worried and upset about many things, but only one thing is needed. Mary has chosen what is better, and it will not be taken away from her." *(Luke 10:38-42)*

There's an important principle to be learned from this passage. If you can't quite figure it out, sharpen up the old brain cells and try this one:

The solution is on page 109.

Jesus Changes Things!

When Jesus looked up and saw a great crowd coming toward him, he said to Philip, "Where shall we buy bread for these people to eat?" He asked this only to test him, for he already had in mind what he was going to do.

Philip answered him, "Eight months' wages would not buy enough bread for each one to have a bite!"

Another of his disciples, Andrew, Simon Peter's brother, spoke up, "Here is a boy with five small barley loaves and two small fish, but how far will they go among so many?"

Jesus said, "Have the people sit down." There was plenty of grass in that place, and the men sat down, about five thousand of them. Jesus then took the loaves, gave thanks, and distributed to those who were seated as much as they wanted. He did the same with the fish.

When they had all had enough to eat, he said to his disciples, "Gather the pieces that are left over. Let nothing be wasted." So they gathered them and filled twelve baskets with the pieces of the five barley loaves left over by those who had eaten.

After the people saw the miraculous sign that Jesus did, they began to say, "Surely this is the Prophet who is to come into the world." *(John 6:5-14)*

What a fabulous experience this must have been for the 5000 guys (not to mention the women and kids) who had come to hear Jesus speak! They learned that Jesus not only had good words, but miraculous powers. Imagine feeding so many with just five loaves of bread and a couple of fish.

It had to be a miracle, 'cause if it wasn't, those loaves and fish had to be pretty BIG! Let's see . . . 5000 men times about six inches of bread per man equals 2500 feet of bread divided by five loaves (carry the nine) . . . uh, that's five loaves at 500 feet each. Eight ounces of fish per mouth . . . 5000 mouths . . . that's two whales each weighing as much as a Toyota. The kid who had brought them for his lunch must have been a hungry dude.

Here's a nifty little brain teaser to remind you that Jesus has the miraculous power to change things. The object is to turn the word at the top of each puzzle into the word at the bottom. You do this by changing one letter at a time, each time forming a new word—a real word. The example below shows you what we mean. In each puzzle we've given you the proper amount of steps to find a solution. However, most puzzles have more than one solution (especially if you use obscure words in the steps, which we've tried to avoid). You may be able to find better answers with fewer steps than we did. We recommend you have a dictionary's help on this one. The words we've chosen for these puzzles come from the Bible passage above. See if you can find where they fit in the story.

Example: Change **WATER** into **WINES**.
(Jesus did that, you know.
See John 2:1-11.)

WATER
_ _ _ _ _
_ _ _ _ _
_ _ _ _ _
WINES

The answer is:

WATER
LATER
LITER
LINER
LINES
WINES

OK, you try it. Jesus changed five loaves into tons. Can you?

FIVE
—— ——
—— ——
—— ——
TONS

Now you're gettin' the hang of it! Here are some more, all from John 6:5-14:

FISH
—— ——
—— ——
—— ——
—— ——
FOOD

BUY
—— ——
EAT

GRASS
—— ——
—— ——
—— ——
PLACE

GAVE
—— ——
—— ——
—— ——
MUCH

MIND
—— ——
—— ——
TEST

GAVE
—— ——
—— ——
—— ——
—— ——
TOOK

LEFT
—— ——
—— ——
—— ——
FILL

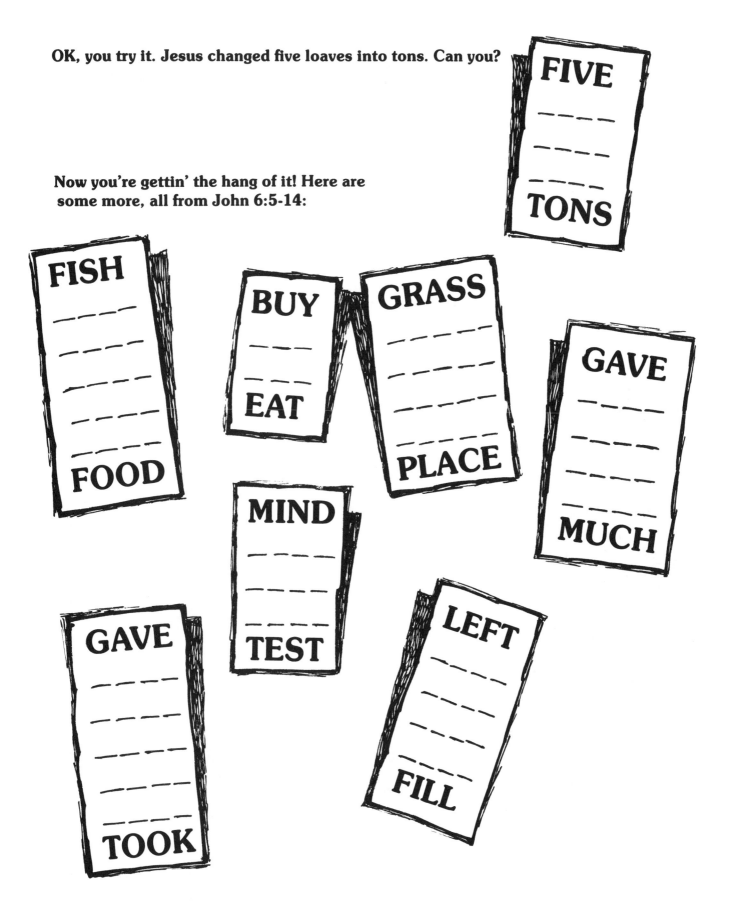

Jesus changes things. Has He changed your life?

Our solutions to the puzzles are on page 109.

Map Zapper!

From this time many of his disciples turned back and no longer followed him. "You do not want to leave too, do you?" Jesus asked the twelve.
Simon Peter answered him, "Lord, to whom shall we go? You have the words of eternal life. We believe and know that you are the Holy One of God."

(John 6:66-69)

Pretty weird, eh? The Lord's disciples started bailing out on Him. Why? Because He was pressing them toward a commitment to discipleship— living fully and completely for Jesus Christ. Being that sort of believer has never been easy.

But Peter hit it right on the head—he and the others who stayed with Christ couldn't think of anyplace better to go. Jesus offered eternal life!

So where did those who deserted Him end up? If you follow the proper directions on the map, you'll find out exactly where they landed.

Instructions: As you can see, the map has been marked with a grid labeled *North, South, East* and *West*. Put the point of your pencil on the small group of ex-disciples near the center of the map. Draw a single line according to the directions printed on the map's legend.

LEGEND:

1. Go North 6 grid spaces.	16. 1 East	32. 3 West	48. 1 East	64. 10 West	80. 5 East
2. 4 East	17. 1 North	33. 1 North	49. 4 North	65. 6 North	81. 1 South
3. 3 South	18. 1 West	34. 5 East	50. 1 West	66. 1 West	82. 2 West
4. 1 West	19. 1 North	35. 2 South	51. 2 South	67. 6 South	83. 5 South
5. 2 South	20. 2 East	36. 1 West	52. 1 West	68. 5 West	84. 5 East
6. 1 East	21. 1 North	37. 1 South	53. 3 North	69. 6 North	85. 4 North
7. 1 South	22. 3 West	38. 1 West	54. 3 East	70. 4 East	86. 2 West
8. 2 West	23. 6 South	39. 1 South	55. 6 South	71. 1 South	87. 2 North
9. 3 North	24. 6 West	40. 1 West	56. 3 West	72. 3 West	88. 1 East
10. 1 West	25. 2 North	41. 1 South	57. 2 South	73. 4 South	
11. 3 South	26. 1 East	42. 3 East	58. 2 East	74. 3 East	
12. 2 West	27. 1 North	43. 1 South	59. 1 North	75. 1 South	
13. 1 North	28. 1 East	44. 10 East	60. 1 East	76. 5 East	
14. 2 West	29. 1 North	45. 3 North	61. 2 South	77. 5 North	
15. 2 North	30. 1 East	46. 1 East	62. 1 West	78. 2 West	
	31. 1 North	47. 2 South	63. 4 South	79. 1 North	

If you're too lazy to finish the game (or if you messed up on the map directions), the solution is on page 109.

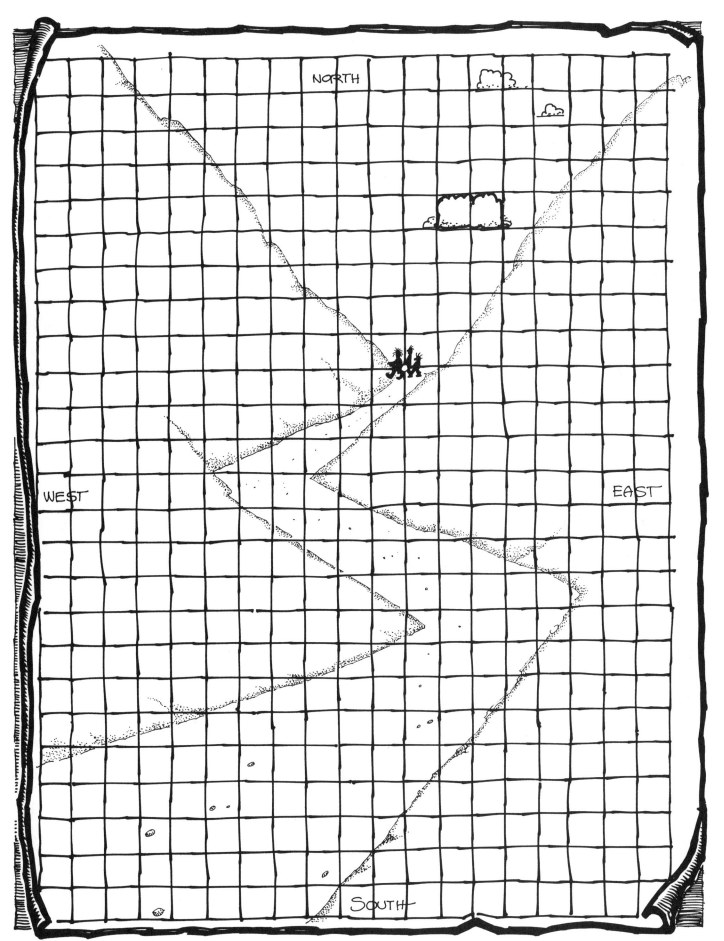

63

What Did He Say?

To the Jews who had believed him, Jesus said, "If you hold to my teaching, you are really my disciples."

(John 8:31)

And if you don't hold to His teaching, you aren't His disciple. Here we have a fun little challenger—are the phrases below things Jesus said or not? Put a check mark next to those you think He said. To find out how well you know His teaching, check the answers on page 110.

1. "All things come to him who waits."

2. "A belligerent child is like a hammer without a head."

3. "Melts in your mouth, not in your hand."

4. "Give to Caesar what is Caesar's, and to God what is God's."

5. "Blessed are the merciful, for they will be shown mercy."

6. "There is a balm in Gilead."

7. "Just say no."

8. "My God, my God, why have you forsaken me?"

9. "Blessed are those who work hard, for they accomplish much."

10. "Man does not live on bread alone."

11. "The light reveals your deepest sins."

12. "When I find myself in times of trouble, mother Mary comes to me."

13. "Anyone who says, 'You fool!' will be in danger of the fire of hell."

14. "Everything is possible to him who believes."

15. "Heaven and earth will pass away, but my words will never pass away."

Don't worry if you have a hard time with this one—the Bible is a BIG book! But those verses you do know, those teachings you have read and heard—you better be living by them if you want to be tight with the Lord!

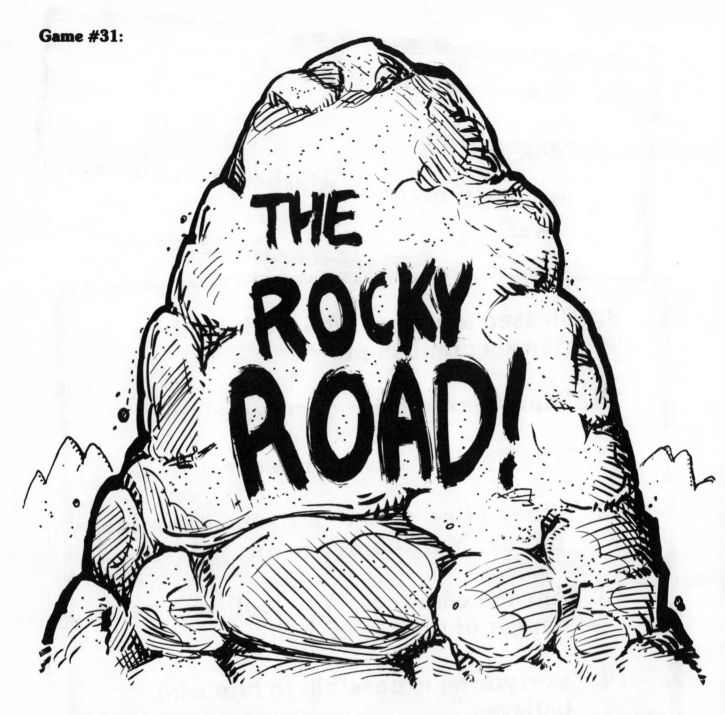

"I tell you the truth," Jesus answered, "before Abraham was born, I am!" At this, they picked up stones to stone him, but Jesus hid himself, slipping away from the temple grounds. *(John 8:58,59)*

When Jesus spoke the words translated in English as "I am," He used a turn of phrase that told His listeners He was claiming to be God. That's why some of them tried to stone Him, for they thought His claim was blasphemy.

By connecting the rocks to the squares (follow the strings) you can spell an interesting observation. Take the first letter of each rock's name and write it in the attached square. Some rocks connect to more than one square.

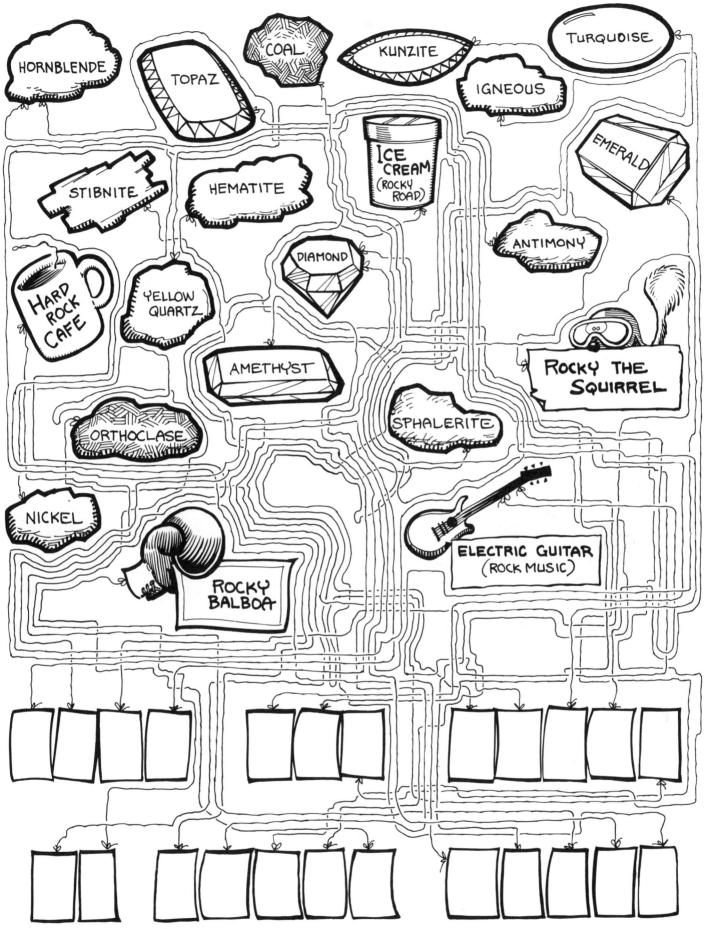

Abundant Life!

"The thief comes only to steal and kill and destroy; I have come that they may have life, and have it to the full." *(John 10:10)*

Jesus came to bring us an abundant life. What does that mean? Some of the many good things that He might provide for anyone are listed on our crazy road map.

Starting at our pal Little Earl, find the route with the most good things on it. End up at the Heavenly Bank. You can't use the same segment of road twice, and you can't cross your own path, except on bridges. If you are playing alone, compare your score to the Score Sheet. You can play against a friend—the winner is the one with the most good things.

See page 110 for a sample score.

69

LIP SERVICE

"These people honor me with their lips, but their hearts are far from me. They worship me in vain; their teachings are but rules taught by men."

(Matthew 15:8,9)

What should happen to people who make the mistake of honoring God only with their lips but not with their lives? Fold along the dotted lines to find out.

Fold so that the arrows meet.

Lip service is a dangerous game. Far too many people think that they can ignore God all week—and please Him by being good on Sunday. God doesn't play that sort of game. He wants us to belong completely to Him. That sort of commitment requires a day-by-day decision to follow God.

THE ANSWER TO THIS SURELY
SHOULD BE FOUND IN THE FOLD
BECAUSE OTHERWISE IT'D LEAVE
MUCH TOO MANY PEOPLE PUZZLED!

The Dirtilizer Crossword!

Jesus called the crowd to him and said, "Listen and understand. What goes into a man's mouth does not make him 'unclean,' but what comes out of his mouth, that is what makes him 'unclean.'

"For out of the heart come evil thoughts, murder, adultery, sexual immorality, theft, false testimony, slander. These are what make a man 'unclean'; but eating with unwashed hands does not make him 'unclean.'" *(Matthew 15:10,11,19,20)*

The people listening to Jesus were hassling Him because His disciples didn't perform a religious ceremonial hand washing before packing down the groceries. As always, Jesus used the situation to make a point: dirty hands don't mean a thing—it's the stuff that comes *out* of the mouth that makes a person grimy.

What sort of stuff? Jesus mentioned some in the passage above and we've thought of several other common "dirtilizers" (things that make you unclean). You can find them in our crossword. Incidentally, here's an extra credit puzzle for you: What is a *cruciverbalist*? Think about it as you work the crossword. The answer is with the game's solution on page 110.

ACROSS

1. Cursing
4. Breaking these is a dirtilizer
7. Bragging
10. Damage (What you can do to a friendship if you say something bad)
12. Tattling
14. A dirtilizer detector
15. Close (Do this to prevent mouth problems)
16. Fury
17. Two words: one falsehood
19. Girl's name (how did this get in here?)
20. These come out of an owl's mouth
21. Hotel (It was dirty when someone told Mary and Joseph there was no room in this)
22. Direct a car (You'll do this away to your friends if you talk too much)
23. Grumble
24. Unclosed (The opposite of what a troublesome mouth should be)
25. Shows response to (Your friend will do this in bad way if your mouth is unkind)
27. Tearful complaint
30. Lendings (Asking for these can cause trouble)
32. Vows (Breaking these causes problems)
34. Regard (What your friends will do if your mouth acts up)
35. Makes a long face

DOWN

2. Overestimation
3. Groove (What you get in if you blab on too much)
5. Squander (What your enemies might do to you if you don't watch your mouth)
6. Vice
7. Boasting
8. Two words: Faithfulness in word only
9. Plenty (Your pals may say this if you keep droning on)
11. Adulations (A *good* thing to do with your mouth)
13. Defamation
18. Criticize
26. Shuts quickly (Excellent idea, O Great Mouth!)
28. Cause injury (Gossip can do this)
29. Wickedness (Lots of ways to do this verbally)
31. Short for reputation (You can lose this fast with a big mouth)
33. Short for south (The direction to head if your mouth gets you in trouble)

73

Who Do  Say?

When Jesus came to the region of Caesarea Philippi, he asked his disciples, "Who do the people say the Son of Man is?"

They replied, "Some say John the Baptist; others say Elijah; and still others, Jeremiah or one of the prophets."

"But what about you?" he asked. "Who do you say I am?"

Simon Peter answered, "You are the Christ, the_____"

(Matthew 16:13-16)

The what? You can find the answer by working your way through this maze. The proper path has the proper words. Other paths also reach the end, but they form wrong answers. The solution is on page 110, but don't cheese out on us.

TIGHT FIT

Then Jesus said to his disciples, "If anyone would come after me, he must deny himself and take up his cross and follow me. For whoever wants to save his life will lose it, but whoever loses his life for me will find it. What good will it be for a man if he gains the whole world, yet forfeits his soul? Or what can a man give in exchange for his soul? For the Son of Man is going to come in his Father's glory with his angels, and then he will reward each person according to what he has done."

(Matthew 16:24-27)

The reward Jesus brings for His faithful disciples is far better than anything that can be gained here on earth. There are some pretty good things here on earth, but what are they compared to the riches of eternal life in heaven? Zippo.

Jesus isn't saying you can't have some of these things—He's saying that they must never become your point in life. We've made a list of things for you to fit into the grid. As in a crossword, the words must correctly share letters. The hard part? It's up to you to figure out where the words go. And some words must go in *backwards* in order to complete the game correctly! (Notice that some of the words are actually two words stuck together so that you can fit them in the grid.) Sound tough? You betcha. The solution is on page 110.

FOOD	POWER	MUSCLES	OILWELLS
LAND	LOOKS	CLOTHES	GOLDMINE
FAME	BONDS	GLAMOUR	CHAUFFEUR
CARS	STOCKS	NOSEJOB	MOVIESTAR
POOL	ESTATE	STABLES	LIMOUSINE
CASH	SILVER	CHATEAU	POPULARITY
GOLD	PEARLS	JETPLANE	ROLLSROYCE
LIMO	CITIES	MANSIONS	SILVERMINE
LUCK	WEALTH	ROCKSTAR	FOOTBALLTEAM
COOKS	JEWELS	SERVANTS	BASEBALLTEAM
MONEY	LUXURY	DIAMONDS	TENNISCOURTS
WORLD	STEREOS	MONEYBIN	

When it comes to possessions, remember one important rule: God cares much more about what we possess on the inside than what we possess on the outside. He wants us to enjoy love, joy, peace, patience, kindness, goodness, gentleness, and a whole bunch of other good stuff—if you don't believe this, read Galatians 5:22,23 for starters.

Amazing Transformations!

After six days, Jesus took with him Peter, James and John the brother of James, and led them up a high mountain by themselves. There he was transfigured before them. His face shone like the sun, and his clothes became as white as the light. Just then there appeared before them Moses and Elijah, talking with Jesus.

Peter said to Jesus, "Lord, it is good for us to be here. If you wish, I will put up three shelters—one for you, one for Moses and one for Elijah."

While he was still speaking, a bright cloud enveloped them, and a voice from the cloud said, "This is my Son, whom I love; with him I am well pleased. Listen to him!"

When the disciples heard this, they fell facedown to the ground, terrified.

(Matthew 17:1-5)

We are used to seeing the human Jesus—a figure draped in robes with long hair, beard, sandals, maybe a donkey. And that's probably the way He looked because that's how everybody looked in those days—'cept the women! (They didn't sport the beards.)

But now for the first time His disciples saw Him as perhaps He appears in heaven. They were stunned. They fell face first into the dirt. Up to that point, the reality of His greatness had not dawned on them—at least not in such a forceful way. His transformation shocked them into understanding who they were dealing with.

In the game business (playing them, that is), transformations can be fun. Perhaps these challenges will help you keep Jesus' real appearance and character in the front of your thinking. The solutions to the first two challenges are on page 110.

Challenge #1: "TRANSFORMING WORDS"

Turn the word at the top of each puzzle into the word at the bottom by changing one letter at a time, each time forming a new word—a real word. One puzzle has a hint.

Becoming a Christian can transform a boy into a man and a girl into a lady:

He can transform hate into love:

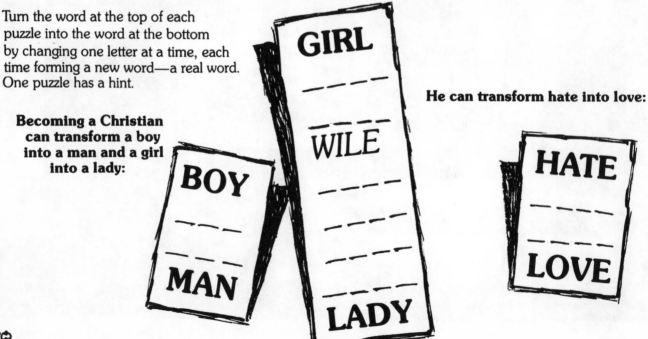

GIRL
____
____
WILE
____
____
LADY

BOY
____
____
MAN

HATE
____
____
LOVE

Challenge #2: "SHE SHUN FAKE LICE TIS HONE"

The strange words in this challenge's title can be transformed to form a phrase taken from the Bible passage on the other page. Six of the verse's words have each been split into two parts and the parts have been shuffled and stuck back together to form the silly words above. You decide where to split the words and how to get them back in the right order. Hint: The phrase concerns Jesus' transformation.

Challenge #3: "HAPPY TO LUAU"

This is an easy one. Fold the page along the dotted lines to form an important message taken from the Bible passage.

Fold so arrows meet, like this:

It's easy for us to forget who we are dealing with when we become followers of Jesus. He's not just some good teacher or nice hero. His transformation proved to His disciples that He is God's Son. Through Him, we are related to Almighty God!

"What do you think? If a man owns a hundred sheep, and one of them wanders away, will he not leave the ninety-nine on the hills and go off to look for the one that wandered off? And if he finds it, I tell you the truth, he is happier about that one sheep than about the ninety-nine that did not wander off. In the same way your Father in heaven is not willing that any of these little ones should be lost."

(Matthew 18:12-14)

The object here is to lead the lost sheep home. However, along the way there are several slight problems, such as ravenous wolves, hungry hunters, bottomless pits and lamb chop fanciers. Your sheep can run into only four of these dangers. If the sheep hits more than four, it becomes somebody's lambskin overcoat.

The Bible passage above explains that God doesn't want any of us to be lost. He has sent Jesus to be our shepherd—He leads us and guides us. If we wander away, we can find ourselves in big trouble. (You might want to spend some time thinking about the spiritual dangers a Christian must sometimes face. Compare the dangers the sheep faces to the ones you face. For example, the poisonous scorpion could represent a certain sin that trips you up.) If you think you may have stumbled away from the Lord, don't wait—ask Him to bring you home again.

The solution is on page 111.

EYE OF THE NEEDLE!

Then Jesus said to his disciples, "I tell you the truth, it is hard for a rich man to enter the kingdom of heaven. Again I tell you, it is easier for a camel to go through the eye of a needle than for a rich man to enter the kingdom of God."

When the disciples heard this, they were greatly astonished and asked, "Who then can be saved?"

Jesus looked at them and said, "With man this is impossible, but with God all things are possible." *(Matthew 19:23-26)*

This game can be played by one or more people. Players each need a coin to use as a marker, a different type of coin for each player. The object is to move your coin from the start up to Heaven.

Put your coin on the start space. Move only one space each turn. Notice that there are large spaces that contain statements such as, "You get your first allowance," and arrows pointing to "Heads" or "Tails." When you land on one of these large spaces, flip your coin to see which arrow to follow. The arrows will lead you either toward or away from the goal. The first person to reach Heaven wins.

This game usually takes a long time to win! In fact, sometimes it *seems impossible* to win—especially when you've been nailed by the "Eye of the Needle" space a time or two.

Jesus made it pretty clear in the Bible passage above: people with possessions are in danger of being weighed down by all their belongings—to the point that they don't have much of a chance of finding eternal life. Why is that? Mainly because rich people often feel no need for God or His salvation. They have the security of their possessions. How poor they really are.

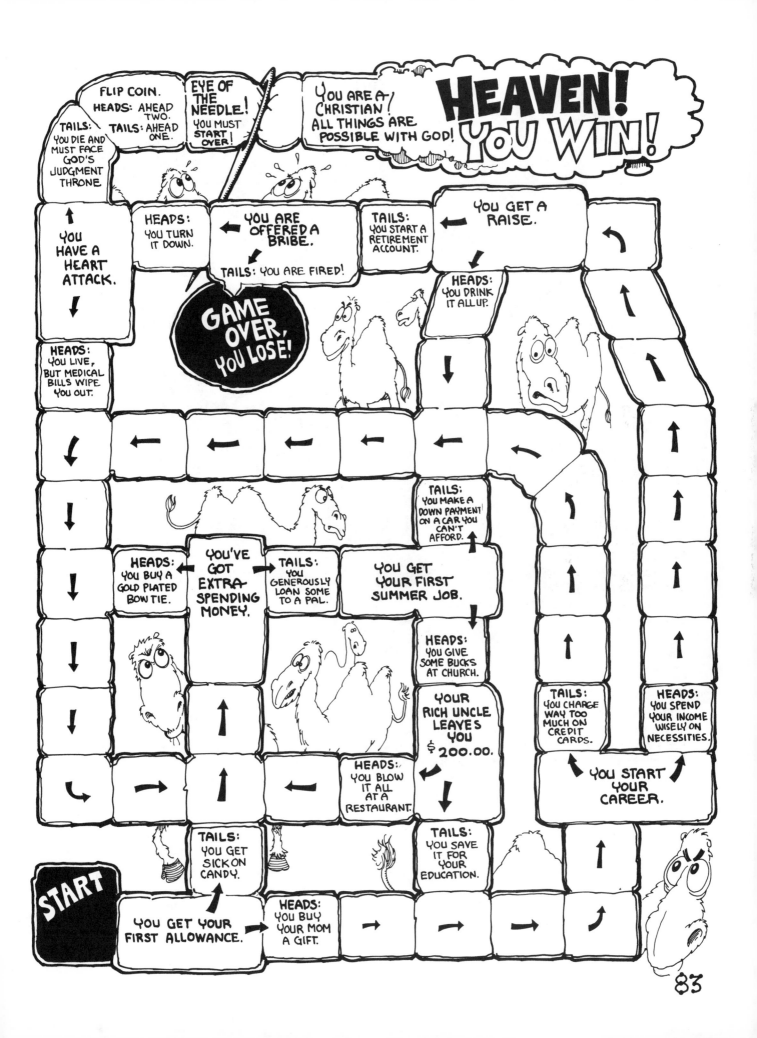

One of them, an expert in the law, tested him with this question: "Teacher, which is the greatest commandment in the Law?"

Jesus replied: "'Love the Lord your God with all your heart and with all your soul and with all your mind.' This is the first and greatest commandment. And the second is like it: 'Love your neighbor as yourself.' All the Law and the Prophets hang on these two commandments."

(Matthew 22:35-40)

This word search game contains exactly 20 practical suggestions for loving God and being friends with others. Each suggestion is a phrase, and each phrase winds through the grid. The phrases can cross each other (sharing a letter). There are no spaces between the words in the phrases, of course. Give yourself one point for each phrase you find, subtract a point for phrases you didn't identify perfectly. The solution is on page 111.

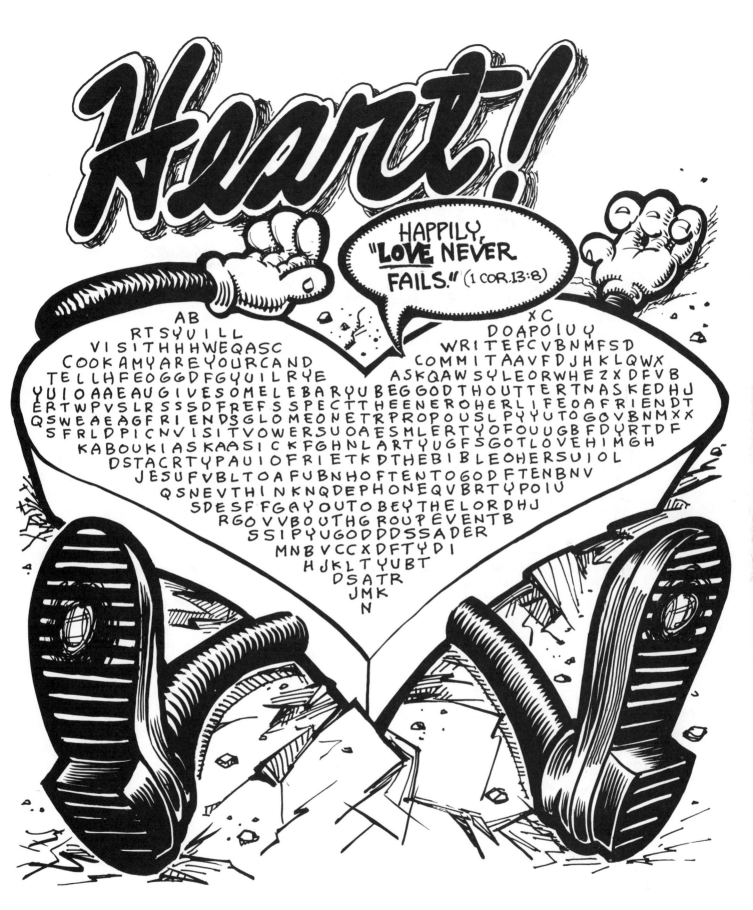

If you follow these suggestions with all your heart, you'll be close to God and have tons of friends!

FOOT RACE!

So he got up from the meal, took off his outer clothing, and wrapped a towel around his waist.

After that, he poured water into a basin and began to wash his disciples' feet, drying them with the towel that was wrapped around him.

When he had finished washing their feet, he put on his clothes and returned to his place. "Do you understand what I have done for you?" he asked them. "You call me 'Teacher' and 'Lord,' and rightly so, for that is what I am. Now that I, your Lord and Teacher, have washed your feet, you also should wash one another's feet. I have set you an example that you should do as I have done for you."

(John 13:4,5,12-15)

Christ set us an example of humble service. He is Lord and King, yet He washed His disciples' feet!

How are you at serving God by serving others? Let's check it out. The questions you see pertain mostly to service projects you could do with your church youth group. (If your youth group has never done these things, you better take that up with your pastor!) Put a check mark in each foot next to the questions that you can answer affirmatively. When you've checked as many feet as you can, add them up and compare your score to the Rating Sheet. Jesus washed 24 feet (assuming each of His 12 disciples had only two)—how many can you get?

Rating Sheet:

21-24: Pedigree!

16-20: Twinkle toes!

11-15: Not bad!

6-10: Pull up your socks!

1-5: Foot odor!

1. Have you ever helped your youth pastor clean a meeting room?

2. Have you ever visited a hospital with your youth group?

3. Have you ever invited friends to a fun youth group event?

4. Have you ever attended prayer meeting and actually prayed?

5. Have you ever given a Bible to anyone?

6. Have you ever helped prepare food for a meeting?

7. Have you ever opened your home to a meeting?

8. Have you ever helped around the church office?

9. Have you ever helped in a car wash or canned food drive?

10. Have you ever set up chairs?

11. Have you ever spoken or sang before the youth group?

12. Have you ever told anyone how you became a Christian?

13. Have you ever told anyone how to become a Christian?

14. Have you ever helped out at your church work day?

15. Have you ever donated something you'd rather keep?

16. Have you ever stopped a fight?

17. Have you ever encouraged a sad or lonely person?

18. Have you ever helped in the little kid's Sunday school class?

19. Have you ever sent a greeting or get-well card to someone?

20. Have you ever assisted an aged or handicapped person?

21. Have you ever made holiday decorations for the meeting hall?

22. Have you ever washed the church bus or van?

23. Have you ever given up the couch to sit on the floor?

24. Have you ever done any of these things without asking to be paid? (Just kidding.)

MANSION MAZE!

"In my Father's house are many rooms; if it were not so, I would have told you. I am going there to prepare a place for you."

(John 14:2)

Jesus has prepared a place in heaven for each of us—some Bible versions say *mansions* instead of *rooms*. Mansions is OK with us!

So let's say it's your very first day in heaven. You've been given the keys to your mansion and—no, wait a minute: no locks in heaven! No bad guys! Anyway, you are trying to get from your front door to your kitchen (just to see what kind of stuff heaven has in the fridge). The mansion's pretty roomy, so lots of luck. The kitchen is marked with a star. The path may take you out on the porch. The solution is on page 111.

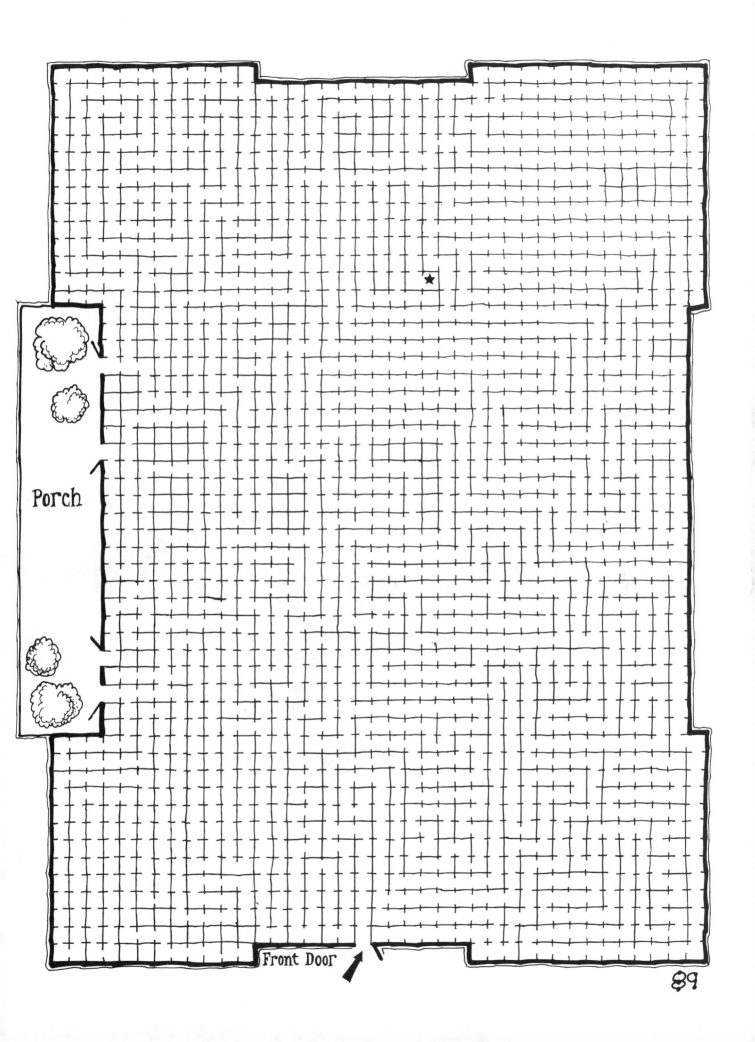

Porch

Front Door

89

Heavenly Maze!

Jesus answered, "I am the way and the truth and the life. No one comes to the Father except through me." *(John 14:6)*

Lots of people try to work their way to heaven by being good. Being good is nice, but Jesus makes it clear that He is the only way to heaven. Without Him, even the best works don't cut it.

The object of the maze is to get to God the Father by way of the three boxes labeled "Way," "Truth," and "Life." However, when you move to any box, the path you take must contain the letters J, E, S, U, S. Only those five letters. The path from the final box to the Father also must spell Jesus. Remember, no one comes to the Father except through Jesus. It is not necessary to go through the three boxes in the order they appear in the Bible verse above, but you must go through all three. The solution is on page 111.

SPIRITUAL GIANTS!

"If you love me, you will obey what I command."
(John 14:15)

How are you at obeying God's commands? Oh. Well, maybe this game will help you out.

Thirty-one of the commands found in the Bible are also found on our game board. Starting at our hero Little Earl, find the route with the most commands on it. End up on the ACME OBEDIENCE METER. You can't use the same segment of path twice, and you can't cross your own pencil line except on paths which obviously don't connect (they cross over and under each other).

There are two things to do to earn points. First, play the game several times until you are sure you've found the path with the most commands. Give yourself one point for each command. Second, give yourself another point for each command you've obeyed (even if your line doesn't go through it). If you spend a few minutes thinking back on specific times you observed these commands, you'll probably end up feeling pretty good—and that makes *us* feel good! Our solution appears on page 111.

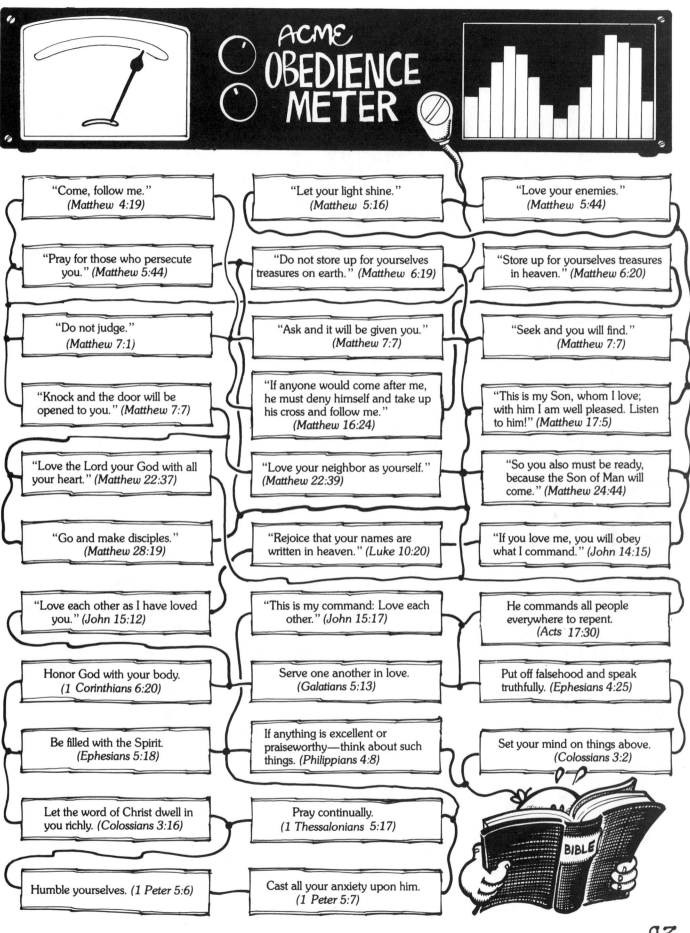

ACME OBEDIENCE METER

"Come, follow me."
(Matthew 4:19)

"Let your light shine."
(Matthew 5:16)

"Love your enemies."
(Matthew 5:44)

"Pray for those who persecute you." (Matthew 5:44)

"Do not store up for yourselves treasures on earth." (Matthew 6:19)

"Store up for yourselves treasures in heaven." (Matthew 6:20)

"Do not judge."
(Matthew 7:1)

"Ask and it will be given you."
(Matthew 7:7)

"Seek and you will find."
(Matthew 7:7)

"Knock and the door will be opened to you." (Matthew 7:7)

"If anyone would come after me, he must deny himself and take up his cross and follow me."
(Matthew 16:24)

"This is my Son, whom I love; with him I am well pleased. Listen to him!" (Matthew 17:5)

"Love the Lord your God with all your heart." (Matthew 22:37)

"Love your neighbor as yourself."
(Matthew 22:39)

"So you also must be ready, because the Son of Man will come." (Matthew 24:44)

"Go and make disciples."
(Matthew 28:19)

"Rejoice that your names are written in heaven." (Luke 10:20)

"If you love me, you will obey what I command." (John 14:15)

"Love each other as I have loved you." (John 15:12)

"This is my command: Love each other." (John 15:17)

He commands all people everywhere to repent.
(Acts 17:30)

Honor God with your body.
(1 Corinthians 6:20)

Serve one another in love.
(Galatians 5:13)

Put off falsehood and speak truthfully. (Ephesians 4:25)

Be filled with the Spirit.
(Ephesians 5:18)

If anything is excellent or praiseworthy—think about such things. (Philippians 4:8)

Set your mind on things above.
(Colossians 3:2)

Let the word of Christ dwell in you richly. (Colossians 3:16)

Pray continually.
(1 Thessalonians 5:17)

Humble yourselves. (1 Peter 5:6)

Cast all your anxiety upon him.
(1 Peter 5:7)

BIBLE

SERVANTS INTO FRIENDS!

"I no longer call you servants, because a servant does not know his master's business. Instead, I have called you friends, for everything that I learned from my Father I have made known to you." *(John 15:15)*

The disciples had been traveling with Jesus for a long time. He knew that His end was near—that He was going to die on the cross and then ascend back into heaven. Before He left, He told His close disciples that they were more than just assistants to Him—they were His pals. We can imagine that this was a moving, emotional experience for the disciples.

The rather strange looking modern day disciples that you see here also want to become Jesus' friends. You can help them by folding the page along the dotted lines as shown in the drawing.

Fold so arrows meet as shown:

The only real way to become Jesus' friend is like this:

"You are my friends if you do what I command" *(John 15:14).*

How's your friendship with the Lord?

Blue-Sky Thinking!

"At that time men will see the Son of Man coming in the clouds with great power and glory. And he will send his angels and gather his elect from the four winds, from the ends of the earth to the ends of the heavens." *(Mark 13:26,27)*

Someday, Jesus will return and, with the help of His angels, gather all the Christians on earth to Him. That's going to be a very unique experience, to say the least!

Here's a fairly tough challenger that might help you practice up for the big day. The object is to connect the star next to the angel in the sky with the star next to Little Earl below. But there is a big catch here: You must use a ruler or other straightedge to draw five connected straight lines from the angel to Little Earl. Your lines must be the same length as the ones shown below. Your lines must be straight, be connected and must not touch any clouds. An example has been done for you. Hint: The lines can cross each other. The solution is on page 112.

Trace these lines, or use a ruler to measure them:

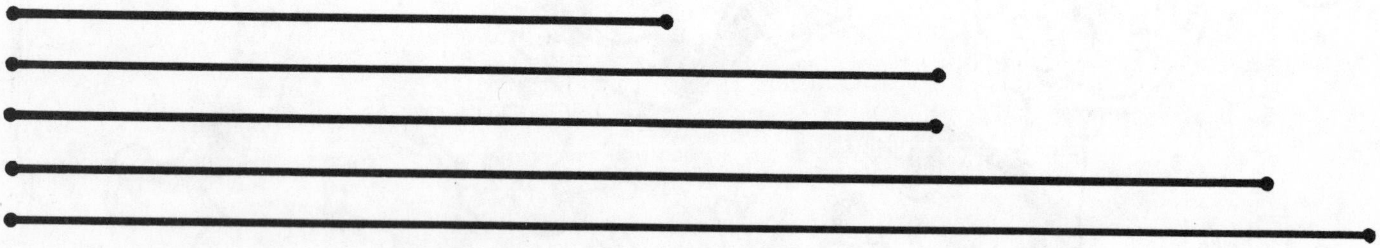

Example game:

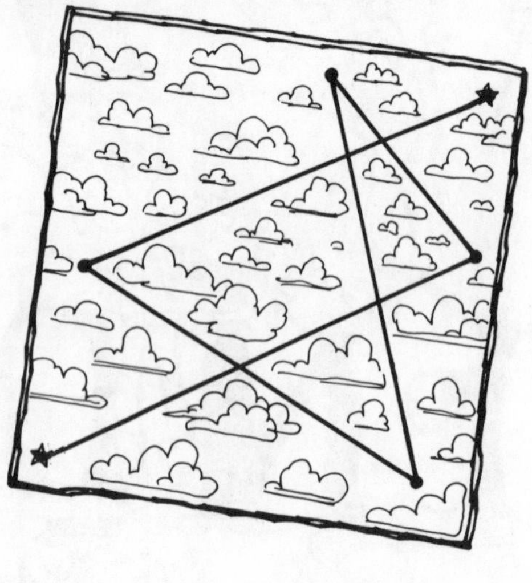

It's exciting to think that someday Jesus will come for us. What will happen to us then? Good things:

Dear friends, now we are children of God, and what we will be has not yet been made known. But we know that when he appears, we shall be like him, for we shall see him as he is.

(1 John 3:2)

"**Therefore keep watch, because you do not know on what day your Lord will come. But understand this: If the owner of the house had known at what time of night the thief was coming, he would have kept watch and would not have let his house be broken into. So you also must be ready, because the Son of Man will come at an hour when you do not expect him.**" *(Matthew 24:42-44)*

When will Jesus return? That's the fun part—nobody knows.

There is a tongue-in-cheek answer to the above question in this word/picture game. You can find it if you solve the puzzle. Just one problem: We dropped the game and broke it! As you can see, many of the pictures are at the bottom of the page. The first part of the puzzle is OK, but to solve the rest of it, you must put the pictures back in proper order—by trial and error. Sound tough? Give it a go and see how you do. But don't make a mistake—who knows what sort of weird message you could find! The solution is on page 112.

Now that you've played the game: Always remember Christ's warning to keep watch. That means to always strive to live for Him and please Him. When He returns, He'll bring His reward with Him.

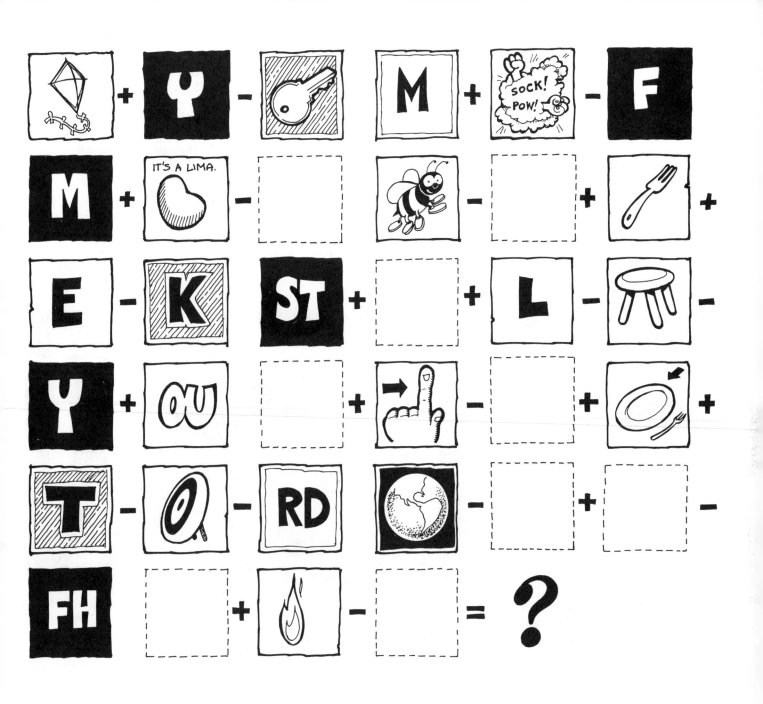

Resurrection Crossword!

As they entered the tomb, they saw a young man dressed in a white robe sitting on the right side, and they were alarmed.

"Don't be alarmed," he said. "You are looking for Jesus the Nazarene, who was crucified. He has risen! He is not here. See the place where they laid him."

(Mark 16:5,6)

This crossword is based on Mark's account of the death and resurrection of the Lord, starting with the night of prayer when He was betrayed by Judas (see Mark 14:32-16:20). Each clue has the Bible verse where you can find the answer. We used the *New International Version*. If you use a different version, some of the words may not be exactly the same. But you should still be able to figure everything out without too much trouble. The solution is on page 112.

ACROSS

3. People who testify. They lied about Jesus (14:63).
8. Accomplished. Jesus did this to the Scriptures (14:49).
10. Proclaim. We are commanded to do so (16:15).

11. One of these long knives cut off the servant's ear (14:47).
13. The place where Jesus prayed (14:32).
15. Boulder used to seal Christ's tomb (15:46).

16. The male offspring of the Blessed One (14:61).
19. Turn over. The women worried about this (16:3).
20. Grief. Jesus felt this (14:34).
24. Sentry. Judas had Jesus led away under this (14:44).
25. Male chicken. It crowed when Peter denied Jesus (14:72).
26. The man who was released in Jesus' place (15:11).
30. Equipped. The crowd that captured Jesus was this (14:43).
31. Not anything. What the women who saw the angel said (16:8).
32. Wailed. Peter did this after he denied the Lord (14:72).
33. The place of burial where they placed Jesus (15:46).
34. Abandoned. The disciples did this (14:50).
35. Accept as true. The disciples didn't accept the word that Jesus was still alive (16:11).
37. Powerful. Jesus sits at this One's right hand (14:62).
39. In contact with. Jesus rose _____ the first day (16:9).
40. Roman soldier. He watched Jesus die (15:39).
44. Not the same. Jesus' other form (16:12).
49. Taken unaware. Pilate was when he heard Jesus had died (15:44).
52. One from Nazareth, like Jesus (14:67).
53. Raised up, like Jesus after his death (16:6).
55. Attesting miracles. The Lord worked these (16:17).
58. Overpowered. Sorrow did this to Jesus' soul (14:34).
61. Escort. The signs do this with those who believe (16:17).
62. Puny. The spirit is willing, but the flesh is this (14:38).
63. Later. Jesus _____ appeared to two disciples (16:12).
66. Passed away. The centurion saw Jesus do this (15:39).
68. Followers of Jesus. He told them to pray (14:32).
70. Expectorate. Some people did this to the Lord (14:65).
71. All. This is possible for the Father (14:36).
72. Another word for body, as in "the spirit is willing but the body is weak" (14:38).
75. The high court of the Jews. They reached a decision (15:1).
77. Courtroom hearing. Jesus went through this in 14:53-65.
79. Between ten and twelve. Jesus rebuked them for unbelief (16:14).
80. Past tense of stand. Some did this as they lied about Jesus (14:57).
81. Garb. What the young man was wearing (14:51).
82. Traveling on foot. Two disciples were doing this (16:12).
83. Christened. Jesus mentioned it (16:16).

DOWN

1. Ruler. Written on the sign fastened to the cross (15:26).
2. The number of demons Jesus drove out of Mary Magdalene (16:9).
3. Inquiry: what reason. The high priest asked this (14:63).
4. Adjacent to, bordering, following. Alluded to in 15:1 regarding the morning.
5. Wrongdoers. Jesus was betrayed into their hands (14:41).
6. Utterances. These did not agree at Jesus trial (14:56).

7. Captive. One was customarily released at the feast (15:6).
9. Troubled. Jesus was deeply this (14:33).
10. Talk to God. Jesus did this at Gethsemane (14:32).
12. Daybreak. The women went to the tomb just after this (16:2).
14. Pained. Jesus was this (14:33).
17. Bludgeon. The crowd had some of these when they arrested Jesus (4:43).
18. Heating. Peter did this in the courtyard (14:67).
21. Penned. The notice of the charge against Jesus was this (15:26).
22. Fettered. What the priests did to Jesus (15:1).
23. Same as #6 DOWN.
24. The Place of the Skull, where Jesus was crucified (15:22).
27. Came in view. Jesus did this to two disciples (16:12).
28. Disavowed. Peter did this regarding Jesus (14:68).
29. Coming along behind. A young man was doing this (14:51).
30. Another word for Father. What Jesus called God (14:36).
36. Entry way. The stone blocked this, the women thought (16:3).
38. Living. The disciples did not believe Jesus was this (16:11).
39. Removed from. The servant's ear was cut this way (14:47).
41. All people. They deserted Him (14:50).
42. Across. The priests handed Jesus _____ to Pilate (15:1).
43. The city where all this took place (15:41).
45. Set foot in. The women did this regarding Jesus' tomb (16:5).
46. Quiet. Jesus gave no answer (14:61).
47. Affirmative. Jesus said this regarding His kingship (15:2).
48. A sour liquid. A man put it in a sponge for Jesus (15:36).
50. Foretell. The people beating Jesus told Him to do this (14:65).
51. Repudiated. Jesus said Peter would do this (14:72).
54. A few, not all of. Several people spit at Jesus (14:65).
57. Planet. We are to go into this to spread the good news (15:15).
59. Labored. The Lord did this with the disciples (16:20).
60. Evil spirit. Seven are mentioned regarding Mary Magdalene (16:9).
64. Belief. Jesus rebuked His disciples for lack of this (16:14).
65. Crying. The disciples were doing this (16:10).
67. Messiah. The priest asked Jesus if He was this (14:61).
69. Clergyman. Mentioned in 14:43.
72. Dropped down. Jesus did this as He prayed (14:35).
73. Singular of #55 ACROSS.
74. Require. The high priest denied this regarding witnesses (14:63).
76. Negative. Jesus said this regarding His rebuilt temple (14:58).
78. Rule, code of ethics. Some were teachers of this (14:43).

Then Jesus came to them and said, "All authority in heaven and on earth has been given to me. Therefore go and make disciples of all nations, baptizing them in the name of the Father and of the Son and of the Holy Spirit, and teaching them to obey everything I have commanded you. And surely I am with you always, to the very end of the age." *(Matthew 28:18-20)*

Your job is to find six words (we won't tell you which) from the Bible passage above to fit in the grid. The words must properly share letters where they cross each other (like a crossword puzzle). When you've found the proper combination, take the letters from the seven shaded areas and write them in the blanks below. We added one letter to make the message complete. If you have the right letters and if you have them in the right order, a message about making disciples will appear. See page 112 for the solution.

__ __ __ __ __ __ __ **G!**

The passage above, Matthew 28:18-20, is known as the Great Commission, because Jesus is commissioning His disciples to tell the world about Him. That job still needs to be done. If you are a Christian, you are responsible to let people know about Him. Sometimes it's hard to get started. Try a little prayer; ask God to help you get on the stick.

We Are All Winners!

After he said this, he was taken up before their very eyes, and a cloud hid him from their sight.

They were looking intently up into the sky as he was going, when suddenly two men dressed in white stood beside them. "Men of Galilee," they said, "why do you stand here looking into the sky? This same Jesus, who has been taken from you into heaven, will come back in the same way that you have seen him go into heaven."

(Acts 1:9-11)

These words from the Bible have a joyous ring to them. Our Lord is coming back someday! If you work all the tricky codes in this game, you'll find a one-word message that sums up the meaning of Christ's return. See if you can find it. If you bomb out, the answers to the various steps are on page 112.

Instructions: First, use this simple code to decipher the encoded crossword puzzle:

A	B	C	D	E	F	G	H	I	J	K	L	M	N	O	P	Q	R	S	T	U	V	W	X	Y	Z
0	!	$	3	@	]	1	4	2	%	&	6	(	)	+	5	9	=	7	?	e	[	;	:	8	⌐

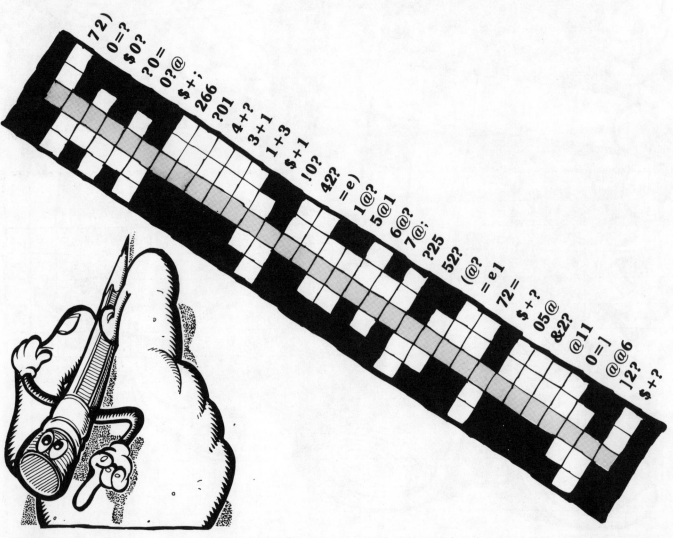

Now write the letters in the grey squares of the crossword grid here:

— — — — — — — —   — — — — —   " — ",   — —

— — — — — — —   — — — — — —   — — — —,

" — — —,"   — — — — — — .

Apply that message to this strange letter (ignore punctuation marks):

DEAR AL:

OUR WEEK WAS EASY, NICE, ETC. I'VE SEEN JO. REST YOUR MIND UNTIL I GET TAMI HELP. AND LOOK, EVEN ONE OF OUR TEACHERS RIPPED ONE.

Write the above message here:

— — — — — —   — — — —   — — — — — —   — —   — — — — —.

Now, using the instructions from the above code, use your pencil to reveal the hidden message in these numbers:

14	83	89	13	23	26	58	67	88	91	127	130	134	140	151	32	47	121	197	187	73	61	16	52	92	101	83
71	129	101	71	181	111	17	172	151	176	13	50	62	175	89	199	121	55	37	20	13	110	125	170	47	51	161
107	156	61	152	173	90	119	164	70	23	31	65	54	121	31	136	125	169	157	97	31	100	137	50	65	105	163
116	99	157	14	44	183	31	41	121	77	133	57	72	144	91	20	112	83	65	61	116	41	80	127	167	78	179
125	78	47	146	197	132	37	62	65	83	121	175	129	167	185	128	31	35	77	124	70	167	199	172	37	114	175
160	36	118	152	136	96	179	87	47	135	195	116	105	31	42	99	108	62	15	150	185	27	20	39	37	117	31
164	147	166	175	179	57	172	21	40	153	20	37	93	50	54	122	45	13	129	50	83	165	13	123	62	171	47
199	195	188	133	154	33	44	18	181	141	70	169	177	73	102	176	111	121	93	37	170	177	80	192	71	24	116
65	21	170	20	155	168	41	126	104	84	170	83	174	91	12	41	135	71	141	176	172	57	139	195	14	91	119
22	49	48	13	120	53	37	117	77	60	39	125	51	77	87	186	72	37	159	113	175	189	105	69	20	81	80
40	53	179	27	31	86	79	175	199	121	107	131	31	172	176	20	109	65	116	101	128	176	71	48	178	41	47
50	122	116	31	83	169	41	125	167	167	185	13	128	91	95	115	31	37	185	128	91	140	62	66	37	13	125
53	167	103	172	145	70	106	89	130	77	142	125	13	101	50	119	125	148	167	71	179	167	20	198	149	160	62
73	113	143	20	62	41	172	37	80	101	121	175	146	158	65	20	37	176	89	125	47	119	41	185	125	178	31

ANSWER SHEETS

#1: The Word!

Jesus is God's trademark on earth.

#2: The Magi Maze!

#5: Believe and Receive!

#6: Snakes Alive!

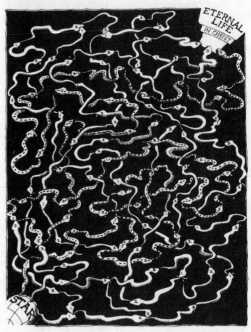

#7: A Fishy Game!

This is the best we could do. Can you do better?

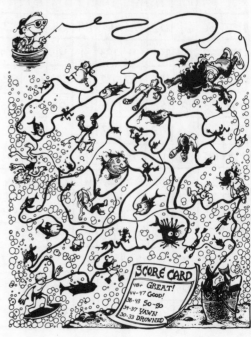

#3: The Next to Impossible Word Search!

EVERYTHING R L J U J K M
R T H X B K F J K L I F W D G O
S EARTH K V N T X S E D F U
O J H G R N K G R O H J T R N
F ANGELS E C E N T T E Q S T
S V B H J I P T Y E F D S A Z V A
PEOPLE I I K S J M N F G F I
W D S W E F R G H J I K D I A N
G R T Y W CLOUDS T C S E S S
G T H U K L O P S Q X C H H K I L
A Q C PLANTS L I E F S D T Y
D F G T J I K O L ANIMALS G
E M T S U M O L P L A S F R Y B H
A O G T STAR ELECTRICITY I
R O H A B K F J K L B X F W D G H
S N T R J ATMOSPHERE F P
O J H S R N K G R E O P H J T R R

106

#8: Crowds and Kinds!

#9: Connections!

There may be more than one solution.

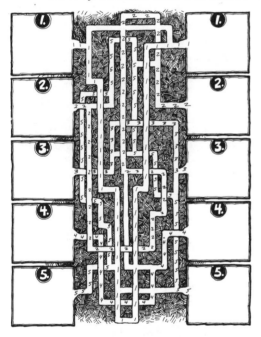

#11: How's That Go Again?

Love is patient. Love is kind. It does not envy, it does not boast, it is not proud. It is not rude, it is not self-seeking, it is not easily angered, it keeps no record of wrongs. Love does not delight in evil but rejoices with the truth. It always protects, always trusts, always hopes, always perseveres. Love never fails.

#13: The Slow Puzzler!

M + ICE CREAM - CREAM + SALT - ICE - MALT = S

HOT + B + FOOD + T + OG - BOOT - HOT DOG = F

DONUT + G - DOG + N - NUN = T

APRICOT - COT + SON + ER - PRISONER = A

The unscrambled answer is FAST.

#18: It's a Gift! There may be other solutions.

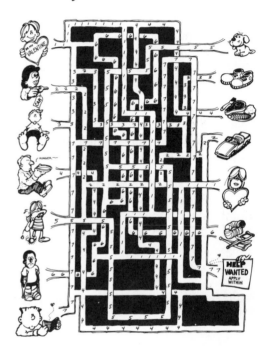

107

#20: Blank Verse!

"Send me some workers,"
 Said the man into the phone;
"It's time to reap the harvest,
 And I'm here all alone."

"Send me Larry, Moe or Curly Joe
 Or anyone you can find;
"I must reap the harvest;
 I'm really in a bind."

"Well now," came the slow reply,
 "Let's see what I can do;
"I'll contact some good workers,
 And send you out a few."

So he got hold of some old guy,
 A friend that he once knew;
But the guy said, "I can't come to work,
 'Cause I'm down with the flu."

He tried again and got in touch,
 With a girl out by the lake;
She would have helped out if she could,
 But she was on her coffee break.

"This is stupid," growled the dude,
 Who decided to be wiser;
But the next clod said, "No, I won't work—
 But I'll be supervisor."

In an angry rage then, this man called,
 Everyone around the nation;
But nobody answered when he called.
 (They were all on a vacation.)

"You must send me someone super quick,"
 said the man out in his orchard;
"If you don't find me someone now,
 I'll see that you are tortured."

So humbly the man bowed and prayed,
 That God would send just any kid;
You can guess what happened next, can't you?
 Just like that He did.

So a little boy arrived for work,
 All happiness and smiles;
Until he took a good look at
 The field, which stretched for miles.

He picked and picked and picked and picked,
 Until the sun turned red;
He piled up the harvest tall,
 Then this is what he said:

"There's way too much to do here,
 More than I can on my own;
"So send me out some workers,
 For I'm here all alone."

#21: Holy Handles!

Peter, Andrew, James, John, Philip, Bartholomew, Thomas, Matthew, James, Thaddaeus, Simon and Judas.

#23: Scrambled Scriptures!

"I tell you the truth, whoever hears my word and believes him who sent me has eternal life and will not be condemned; he has crossed over from death to life." *(John 5:24)*

"I tell you the truth, a time is coming and has now come when the dead will hear the voice of the Son of God and those who hear will live." *(John 5:25)*

Salvation is found in no one else, for there is no other name under heaven given to men by which we must be saved. *(Acts 4:12)*

Today, if you hear his voice, do not harden your hearts. *(Hebrews 4:7)*

Therefore, there is now no condemnation for those who are in Christ Jesus. *(Romans 8:1)*

All Scripture is God-breathed and is useful for teaching, rebuking, correcting and training in righteousness, so that the man of God may be thoroughly equipped for every good work. *(2 Timothy 3:16,17)*

For the word of God is living and active. Sharper than any double-edged sword, it penetrates even to dividing soul and spirit, joints and marrow; it judges the thoughts and attitudes of the heart. *(Hebrews 4:12)*

#24: The Cost of Discipleship!

#25: It Was a Dark and Stormy Night!

(SPLAT!)

#26: The Name Game!

B + BOY + WELL - BOWL + L - BELL +
  POOL + ICE - POLICE + FUR - F = YOUR

P + NAIL + L - PILL + DIME - DIE + E = NAME

KISS - KS = IS

GEM + YSER - GEYSER + LOUD +
  VE - LOVE = MUD

#27: Martha, Martha, Quite Contrary

KNEE + GIFT - NET - KEG = IF

BOY + W - BOW + O + HOUSE - HOSE = YOU

JARS + NET - JET + ELEVEN - SEVEN - NL = ARE

BOW + TOOLS - BOWLS = TOO

TU + WEB + BULL - WELL - TUB + APPLES -
  APPLE + Y = BUSY

COFFEE + T - FEET + P - COP + DOOR + T - DOT = FOR

BAG + T - BAT + TOAD + POLE - TADPOLE + D = GOD

SKY + I - SKI + COUCH + APE - CAPE - CH = YOU

HAIR + TEN - HIT - N = ARE

W + SANTA + D - SAND + CARROT - CAR -
  WART + O = TOO

BUS + Y = BUSY

#28: Jesus Changes Things!

There are undoubtedly many possible solutions to these puzzlers.

FIVE	**FISH**	**BUY**	**GRASS**	**GAVE**	**MIND**
FINE	FIST	BUT	GRADS	GATE	MINT
FINS	MIST	BAT	GRADE	MATE	TINT
TINS	MOST	**EAT**	GRACE	MATH	TENT
TONS	MOOT		GRACE	MACH	**TEST**
	MOOD		GLACE	**MUCH**	
	FOOD		**PLACE**		

GAVE	**LEFT**
LAVE	LIFT
LACE	GIFT
LACK	GILT
LOCK	GILL
LOOK	**FILL**
TOOK	

#29: Map Zapper!

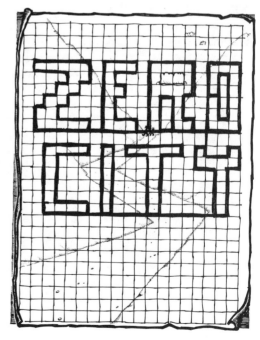

#30: His Teaching!

4. "Give to Caesar what is Caesar's, and to God what is God's." Luke 20:25

5. "Blessed are the merciful, for they will be shown mercy." Matthew 5:7

8. "My God, my God, why have you forsaken me?" Mark 15:34

10. "Man does not live on bread alone." Matthew 4:4

13. "Anyone who says, 'You fool!' will be in danger of the fire of hell." Matthew 5:22

14. "Everything is possible to him who believes." Mark 9:23

15. "Heaven and earth will pass away, but my words will never pass away." Mark 13:31

#32: Abundant Life!

This is the best we could manage. Can you do better?

#34: The Dirtilizer Crossword!

A cruciverbalist is someone who does crossword puzzles.

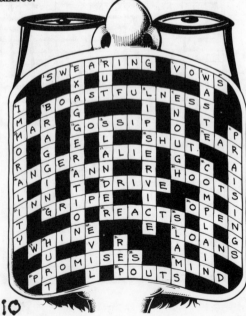

#35: Who Do You Say?

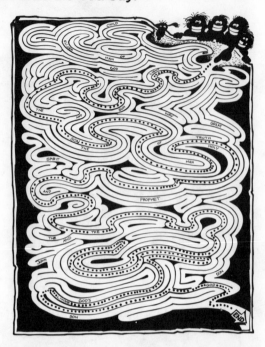

#36: Tight Fit!

#37 Amazing Transformations!

Challenge #1:

BOY	GIRL	HATE
BAY	GILL	HAVE
BAN	WILL	HOVE
MAN	WILE	LOVE
	WIDE	
	WADE	
	WADS	
	LADS	
	LADY	

Challenge #2: HIS FACE SHONE LIKE THE SUN.

#38: The Wild and Wooly Maze!

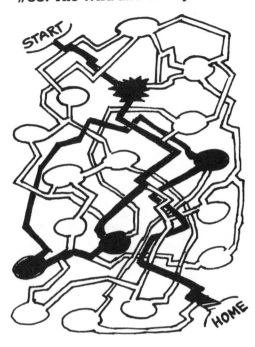

START

HOME

#40: All Your Heart!

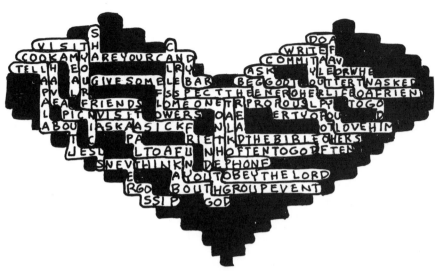

#42: Mansion Maze!

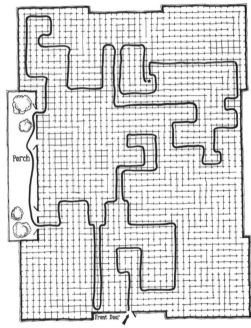

Porch

Front Door

#43: Heavenly Maze!

#44: Spiritual Giants!

This is as many as we could get. Can you do better?

WAY

TRUTH

LIFE

#46: Blue-Sky Thinking!

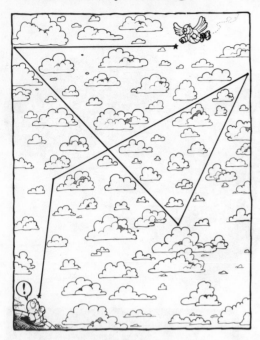

#47: Watch Out!

KITE + Y - KEY = IT

M + FIGHT - F = MIGHT

M + BEAN - MAN = BE

BEE - E + FORK + E - K = BEFORE

ST + YO-YO + L - STOOL - Y + OU = YOU

STAR + FINGER - S + DISH + T - TARGET - RD = FINISH

EARTH - EAR + FISH - FH = THIS

BAG + FLAME - BAFL = GAME

#48: Resurrection crossword!

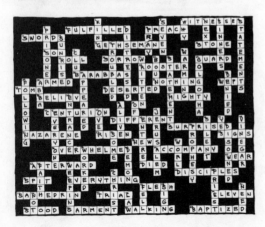

#49: Grey Areas!

GET GOING!

#50: We Are All Winners!

The crossword:

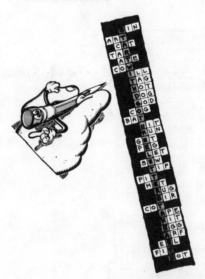

SIN	LET
ART	SEW
CAT	TIP
TAR	PIT
ATE	MET
COW	RUG
ILL	SIR
TAG	COT
HOT	APE
DOG	KIT
GOD	EGG
COG	ARF
BAT	EEL
HIT	FIT
RUN	COT
GET	
PEG	

The crossword spells **START WITH "D," GO THREE LETTERS, TAKE "A," ETC.**

The message from the letter is **DARKEN EVERY MULTIPLE OF THREE.**

The darkened numbers reveal this message:

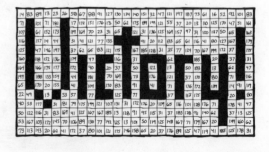

112